Beyond Awareness is .....
The Land of Forces

Dr. Liana Mattulich

Copyright © 2025 Dr. Liana Mattulich.

All rights reserved. No part of this book may be reproduced, stored, or transmitted by any means—whether auditory, graphic, mechanical, or electronic—without written permission of both publisher and author, except in the case of brief excerpts used in critical articles and reviews. Unauthorized reproduction of any part of this work is illegal and is punishable by law.

ISBN: xxx-x-xxxxxxx-x-x (sc)
ISBN: xxx-x-xxxxxxx-x-x (hc)
ISBN: xxx-x-xxxxxxx-x-x (e)

Because of the dynamic nature of the Internet, any web addresses or links contained in this book may have changed since publication and may no longer be valid. The views expressed in this work are solely those of the author and do not necessarily reflect the views of the publisher, and the publisher hereby disclaims any responsibility for them.

WARNER PUBLISHING

369 Lexington Ave 3rd floor
New York, NY 10017

CONTENTS

Forward: Feeding the Birds vii
Welcome From Dr. Liana x

Chapter One: Human Inner Keys for Evolution 1

Awareness
Self-Healing
Human Potentials
Wisdom Tools
Introspection
Story, 'Rat in the Dojo'
Metaphors, Axis, Safe Place, Letting Go, Immune Response
Sensory Integration, CATS, Self-Healthy Pathways
Analogies
Symbols
Sounds
Art, Reading, and other Creative Acts
Journal

**Chapter Two: Technology of Neuro-Biofeedback in Human
Inner Keys for Evolution** 28

Methodology for Use Self Neuro-Biofeedback Sessions
Principal Training Sites
First Primordial Concept
Second Primordial Concept
Third Primordial Concept
Fourth Primordial Concept

"You Have the Right to Change Your Mind"
Changing Biochemistry by Changing Physiology
Grounding, Axis, CATTSK, 3 Legs
Observer as Human Possibility to Regain Healthy Long Life

Chapter Three: Eastern Wisdom: Points and Bridges in the Morphologic Field 41

Eastern-Oriental Wisdom of Acupuncture Points
Eastern Medicine in Modern Times
Meridians, Extra Meridians, Assembler Points, Attractor Area
Second Skin, Bridges at the Morphologic Field, Portals
Tapping and Tips for Fast Successful Outcomes
4 Gates, Third Eye, Upper Lips, Ear, Thymus
Story: 'If You Know How to Breath You Know Eternity'

Chapter Four: Recognition of Useful Energies for Self-Healing, Self-Regulation, Self-Evolution Using the Enneagram as a Universal Map 58

Basic Concepts
Enneagram as Map of the Human Alchemy, Inner Work of Self-Transformation
Energies 768 / 384 / 192
First Trace, Owner a Healthy Life
Energies 96 / 48 / 24
Second Trace, Owner with Success Your Personal Goals
Energies 12 / 6 / 3
Third Trace of Self-Evolution Beyond Awareness
Poem: 'The Ancient Language'

Chapter Five: Motor Sensory Integration, Exercises, Movements and Tools 70

Exercises, Tools, and Movements
Methodology for Integrate Quality of Energies by Exercises, and Movements
Three Legs Position
Exchange Exercise
Sweeping Exercise
Tools for Building Awareness, Presence, 'Higg' Will
Spatial Movements
Gathering and Grounding Cords
Sound Practices for Dream-Works
Walking Warrior

Tu Sho
Story of Personal Application

Chapter Six: Seven Somatic Systems, Seven Minds, Seven Brains and Mathematical Correlations 89

Psychophysiology of Seven Biologic-Somatic Systems
Psychophysiology of Seven Minds in Awareness and Beyond
Psychophysiology of Seven Brains in Awareness
Modern Times
Success at Personal Goals and Self-Expansion into Universal Field
Innovations Transform Impossible Things in Efficient Outcomes with Inner Joy
Story: A Tale of Motivation, 'Froggie and Buffo Frogs.

Chapter Seven: Evolution is Applying Cosmic Order in Daily Life 103

Practice Order with Mathematical Proportions
Key Words Meaning
Claustrum Neurons Data
Synopsis and Review of Connecting the Dots to Reach Self-Goals

Glossary 114
Biographies and Contact us 125
Appendix with Graphic Illustrations 129

Forward

The Metaphysics of Feeding the Birds at Liana's Home: Thirty Years of Learning Practical Applications of Matter Energy Forces

Thirty years ago, I wrote a story about drinking mate, while watching the birds and squirrels in Liana's yard. The take away lesson from that story was that when I pause to savor and connect with the daily rhythms of nature, it gives me insight and preparation to navigate my daily interactions with humans.

I now write to share recent learnings from time spent at Liana's Mountain home.

I was asked to feed the birds in a specific way. Place three different types of food in differing amounts in differing places. Each quantity and location of food was based on the quality-of-life supporting nutrition that was being offered.

The majority of the food that I placed first location consisted of left over bread and other food scraps. It was placed in an open metal dish. Easily seen and accessed, this food represents the quality of everyday life nourishment. Metaphysically known as "matter", within health system this is, known as body. The second smaller portion of food was a block of suet. A little harder to find and requiring more work to produce this form of food, this food provides broader nutrition to support life. This represents the "energies" that flow in and through us to support our life.

The third and smallest portion of food that I placed was birdseed. This required more effort for the birds to find and consume and represented the metaphysical distillation that we call "forces."

In addition to review of matter/energy/forces, the lesson of proportions is also important. As you read more in this book you will find terms like dominant (approximately 2/3); complement (approximately 1/3) and minimum of minimum (small portion acts like catalyst). This is related to phi ratios. If we look at western culture, we get stuck with the idea that balance equals 50:50. This is a very static way of dancing with life. We see this phi ratio of proportions in our everyday world. In matter and art, it shows up as the Fibonacci spiral.

Also, either by coincidence or simultaneous synchronicity, the same year that I met Liana I started to teach medical acupuncture. Creating order out of this plastic doll that had lines with organ names drawn from head to foot, I had to think about what I knew about our bodies. How to unite the differing ways of describing human function? The answer is…FASCIA. The meridians/channels overlayed fascial planes.

To create WHOLE HEALTH with the integration of western medicine – with focus on matter and structure, and eastern medicine – with focus on energy and flow, we need both. Like our skull brain theoretically has a left –linear side, and a right –holistic side, both contribute to the whole. While we are looking at this integration of western and eastern health. Have you noticed that the chakras all overlie hormone producing glands?

I have known and worked with Liana for 30 years. In our first meeting in 1995 she used biofeedback technology to show me that my meditation practice of 20 years was a practice of dissociation. I was not actually producing any positive physical mental or physiologic benefits. YIKES and OUCH, twenty years wasted!

I started studying with her at that time. Over the years our relationship has evolved to include deep friendship. I found a fellow physician committed to the same path of integrating western and eastern health with metaphysics and quantum physics.

During my tenure at University of Maryland Center for Integrative Medicine, while teaching physicians the importance of applying physics to the idea of health care, I would show a rectangle with Newtonian physics in the lower right corner, and quantum physics in the upper right corner. Newtonian physics applies everyday observations. Do you remember the story of the apple hitting Newton on the head? In contrast quantum physics applies to the realms of very small and very large, requiring a different way of looking at the universe. As I sat side-by-side with Liana to edit this book, I held the intention to maintain the cadence of her voice in the written words. As you read the words on the book's pages, absorb the information with all of your being, not just your eyes and intellectual mind. For Liana to create this book required decades of life experience that blends:

Lyrical Spanish, linear English, science, wisdom stories, transcendental wisdom, art, neuroscience, physics, language beyond language, and MORE. It required a holistic approach to write and will require a holistic approach to read and then apply and live. :o)

Liana helps me do that. This book will help you do that.

Thank you in advance for your consideration and respect. Enjoy the journey.

Sharon Montes MD

Founder Living Well Whole Health

Welcome Words from Dr. Liana

This book started in 1995, as Beyond Awareness is ... now, updated and in the new cycle of seeds of wisdom for high evolution, is called:

Beyond Awareness is ..... The Land of Forces

This is the review of the information with modern eyes and the great lucky news that scientific technology is now capable to do what we 'dreamed about' 30 years ago.

Also, know that this book only begins to open a very broad ancient wisdom that meets modern scientific research. This blending has been proven to help people enjoy their birthright of having a longer healthier life, plenty in self-regulation success with inner joy.

YES!!! ... It is possible Now-Here by yourself.

Human Inner Keys for Evolution / HIKE4evolution is only a socio-cultural name needed in modern legal status. The team of professionals in many branches of science, plus the synchronistic places of actions with simultaneity in the goals of evolving planetary peace, with respect for life and pristine principles, are moving with perfect cadence.

Many years ago, my friend, David, MD, in Hawaii asked:

"Why read this book? To explore your mind and your reality because you want more than you commonly experience."

Maybe you ask: Why is this book in my hands? Here-Now is the right space-time for a new generation of intelligent people to dialog-discuss out of the box ideas, which opens possibilities of increasing the quality of personal life. Now you can self-heal dysfunctional patterns imposed on you, and restore your birthright to enjoy wellbeing and a long life.

Synthetizing ancient wisdom and modern science in a format of pages, is it a somewhat ridiculous attitude. However, here we are! This book contains the tools that allow you to be the owner of awareness united with optimal performance and self-healing.
With this information you can integrate psycho-physiologically processes in simultaneously presence at the level of cellular immune system, and developing those in a self-regulating reality of body-mind-energies-soul-fields-forces. Shining from yourself… to yourself.

Give me a few moments of your precious time and I assure you: this healing journey of flying together will be a win-win-win reality!
Everyone starts in kindergarten… The magic place where we play together with others in joy, learning new skills. Growing healthy naturally involves taking new information and connecting it like a neckline/collar of pearls. Like layers of an onion, we expand the depth of our dimensionality where subtle potentials open.

This book is organized for you to learn and own your birthright of BE… The chapters are basic files to accomplish enough information of specific pieces of the puzzle; once the last page is read, your psychophysiology understood, with the help of your intellectual mind. It is time to execute, engage, and embrace the journey.

Execution is only possible from you to you. Cognitive information without involving the somatic body, energetic fields, and aware volitive mind, is only to have a map of a destination. Now is needed to walk the distance. Olympic do more that running, they become athletes. HIKE4Evolution™ system is a sendero luminoso / light pathway of self-development of higher optimal potentials, which by open perceptions bring what you want to success!

Engage yourself in this puzzle and move-on without direct human support maybe scary you? The good news is: in the HIKE4Evolution™ system it is a wonderful gift, the teamwork. First, participants counted with an incredible amount of wisdom accessible by the internet web guide.

Second, teamwork develops in time when is commitment from the participants. Excellent human beings, professionals in health care, and masters at specific topics intertwining the fabric of this different style of learning to learn how, and when to easily manifest your goals.
Here some few examples:

A young professional with mastery in self-evolution which, with agape, oxytocin, and a lot of experience in resolving problems, and passing obstacles, teaches excellent tips to fast apply precise tools of awareness on right momentum. She is with you all the time that you need to develop this learning process of self-health with gratitude and acceptance on your daily life, and success!
This is her short biography for your information. Alistair M. Hawkes, MA, LPC

Alistair M. Hawkes is a licensed psychotherapist who specializes in guiding fellow therapists, art professionals, and corporates executives to find inner peace and higher dynamic creativity to fly beyond awareness, using the HIKE4evolution™ system. She is passionate about helping others, persistent in a fault, and loves to learn.

Alistair is available for stage speaking and media interviews. She loves to share on topics that focus on providing these leaders with actionable insights and tools to address and prevent burnout, and distress, creating their best lives. This ensures they can continue to provide effective outcomes and success, while maintaining their own well-being.

When the alchemy transformation is your next opportunity, will be another young master, which with highest compassion (does not use band aid but is one 'expert' on amputation quickly any gangrenes), offered efficient outcomes with his humble presence of never ending wisdom. As teamwork global coordinator opens to your goals new fountains of unique vivencias, practices, movements, etc., which the system offers worldwide.

This is his short biography for your information. Dallas R. Hawkes, M.S. - Applied Mathematics

Dallas Hawkes is an ordinary man. As a long-time seeker of a deeper understanding of the power of faith, logic and intent, Dallas has been a student of various martial arts and body movement systems, Native American prayer services and mathematics. Body movement helped create healthy boundaries and flexibility. Mathematics taught abstract thought. Spending time with the original people of this land integrated the importance of community, where real change happens, if dedicated.

He has been highly trained in the use of bio-neurofeedback by Dr. Liana Mattulich, MD (Argentina), pioneer on scientific feedback to open 'wings' -human higher potentials.

Using technology in ways taught by the HIKE4Evolution™ system has accelerated the integration of many experiences of his life leading to a clear, sustainable vision of becoming more humane together.

As a bonus gift, when the participant is doing the system in the order and cadence efficient for the personal goals declared, they will start some proportion of Dream-Works. Read the first story and you will understand. Beyond a physical photo of myself, or avatar, or hallucinations of instant gratification, I am only one….. 'Sleeping Cat.'
Embrace the journey, please. It is your birthright. It is a blueprint that lives in your stem cells, knowing, and manifesting reality based on the cosmic value of highest evolution: BE healthy, efficient in your environment, and radiate a genuine joy here-now.

If you are an advanced master that opens this book, this is the right space-time for you to have the highest open perceptions, because with your previous studies, now you are capable of reading the blue print of the basic tools of the system. For 50 years I brought this information with the hope that someone, someday, like you today, catch this unique opportunity with new eyes, to read, and to create the 'Higg Reality' (1) here-now of Be, Soy, Estoy……. Such as, from that tingling that your hands perceived in the beginning of your research to when exchange exercise harmonizes your arms movements or, that yummy taste signal so deep when the clock exercise shines your second skin…

(1)--- 'Higg' information-energy 768 in quantic potential, allows new layers of creations self-regulated, which manifest healthy and efficient outcomes with radiant inner joy in self-freedom…..

Now you are the owner of the wisdom of your psychophysiological reality, and it is in your power to decide how High /'Higg' you want to BE, in total freedom from any dependency.   When solar photons touch assembler points on your body, your microtubules vibrate as light. You then experience in the cellular cytoplasm (tingly hands), or a taste perception (yummy texture) is now nourishment flowing as river of Qi / Ki in the multiple realities of your presence, body-minds-energies-fields-forces… When Observers are capable of real discernment, creativity flourishes with the original smile…..

This healing journey of flying together will be a win-win-win reality
Beyond Awareness is….. The Land of Forces
Welcome……… Liana

CHAPTER ONE

Human Inner Keys for Evolution

Life in modern societies has evolved dramatically over the past decades along two parallel, but potentially conflicting paths. The first is the literal explosion of sophisticated, hand-held technologies that enable almost anyone to access information, about anything from anywhere at any time, from an ever-expanding knowledge base to advance their formal learning, personal fulfillment, and quality of life.

The second path includes a growing number of people who desire to expand their cognitive consciousness to awareness and beyond, to optimize their psycho-physiological potentials to the fullest in all aspects of their lives – sometimes through the use of bio-neuro-feedback technologies – but without hitting "the techno-saturation wall" and sacrificing their overall wellbeing in the process.

As a medical doctor, I dedicated the first part of my life to working with and researching humans who were expressing their inner powers in daily life. From masters of martial arts, lamas with proven reincarnations, and Sufi wisdom, I collected data from brainwaves, plus psychophysiological (mind-body-energy) information. This tapestry of life observed in different places around the world, South America, Europe, USA, etc. showed interesting similarities and synchronistic signals that allowed me to draw maps of states of consciousness, and beyond. The system that I created during these 50-years of parallel professional and personal inner work today is called Human Inner Keys for Evolution (HIKE).

The HIKE system of training allows fast achievement of goals such as:

- optimizing potential in all aspects of daily life;
- reducing stress;
- enhancing mental focus and functioning;
- being more creative in their careers and leisure pursuits;
- optimizing mindfulness;
- increased imagination and problem-solving abilities;
- in everyday life, contributing productively to a harmonious, sustainable quality of life on the planet.

The HIKE system helps you accomplish these goals through using home-based self-training with biofeedback and neurofeedback. Our unique software is available only through one vender. This technology is blended with a wide range of ancient wisdom tools and the precise details of proven integrative movements. This synergistic approach efficiently interconnects all aspects of our mind-body-energies-fields-forces.

Specifically HIKE training includes:

- EEG Neurofeedback (NF) is used (up through high gamma brainwave frequencies at 250 Hz) in unique way, to achieve increasing and optimizing body-mind-energies functioning. This is much faster and sustainable than classic "consciousness-expanding" methodologies. Unlike other traditions said, we KNOW that alpha training isn't the highest possibilities in optimal performance.
- From cognitive consciousness is possible to develop a consistent level of awareness, sustainable on daily optimal performance with wisdom. Awareness is a high human state NOT related to alpha brainwaves, but to neuronal gamma synchronicity plus slow cortical potential (glias), in self-regulated harmony with energy fields opens at mathematical proportion.
- Using acupuncture / tapping on a few key cranial meridian points (which western practice known as Cz, F3, F4, P3, and P4) to boost EEG training's create beneficial effects, and accelerate the learning of a best psycho-physiologically quality of life, harmonic to personal goals. We also use a few selected body meridian points to augment the results.

- Integrating a combination of exercises and movements grounded in various Yoga, Sufi, South American shamanic traditions, Taoist, and Martial Arts; these practices increase inner joy and vitality.
- "Ancient wisdom tools" of Introspection, Stories, Analogies, Metaphors, Sounds, Symbols, and Sensory Integration are used.
- To open doors of perceptions the system is using metaphors, analogies, and stories --drawn from diverse worldwide wisdom traditions and eminent figures such as Lao Tzu, Idries Shah, Anthony de Mello, and Edward de Bono.
- In HIKE is applying a range of sounds and symbols that have both eastern / oriental and western roots (e.g., the voices of real animals --such as whales; specific oriental bells; sounds of the vibrational fields of the planets on the solar system --recorded by the two NASA-Voyages; and nature elements) to lightly stimulate and synchronize the brain's hemispheres.
- Offering additional "home study" practices like journaling, art, and selected readings designed to ground brain plasticity and sustain progress in areas important for achieving participants' personal goals.

Human Inner Keys for Evolution is an innovative self-development path of intertwined ancient wisdom practices with modern technology, ready to help you regain your human potential to be happy, efficient meeting challenges, and live in state of wellbeing.

With few weeks of practices, you will discover a new quality of freedom from the heavy burden of trash from the past and will develop self-regulated states of energies that open physical vitality, mental plasticity with a precise discernment of what you really want beyond the sociocultural pressures. Using the modern technology of feedback will save time and give you the best results.

This is an invitation to take a Journey Beyond Awareness. Each chapter will focus on the tools needed to obtain fast results. The integrative map is easy synthetize by symbolic forms that giving cadence, common sense structure, and open perceptions in creation of ideas, projects, goals as you want, but also, manifest these abstract concepts in tangible form, with molecular texture, at daily life.

"May the Force be with you" is a line from a movie and TV series... Cognitive conscience is the land of intelligent people.
Awareness is the human potential to be our own field of forces as Observer, such as in the cat experiment of modern science, where always the Observer 'defines' the outcomes (Schrodinger cat)... Welcome .....

Wisdom Tools

Human Inner Keys for Evolution (HIKE) presents your learning material in a specific order, based on modern scientific information.
How, when, what and why to learn are the foundations that gives our system sustainable fast outcomes aligned with the individual goals that the participant wants. The system teaches effective biological tools that mentally and energetically activate each individual's psycho-physiology – aka mind-body pathways.
Results are optimized through the synergistic commitment of the entire team: taking some "pieces or parts" without the deep connections between them, will not render the same results. The totality of the inner journey is more than the sum of the miles. Mapping the entire physiology extends far beyond neurofeedback training alone. The human body is more than matter.

In the physiology of energetic components, the electric realm of human nervous system is the most accepted in science, but the subatomic fields, electromagnetic connections, and effects in the psychophysiology of people correlated to gravitational forces (solar storms, supernovas, collision of distant stars of this universe, etc.) are the advanced studies on optimal performance that open the 'wings' (symbolic analogy) of BE all that you want to BE.

Introspection

HIKE4evolution applies a natural flow of daily events to practice "presence ..." As in Zen the path to enlightenment is to 'cut wood, carry water' everything provides an opportunity to jump from cognitive consciousness to a subtle different and sustainable reality, Awareness.

When human physiology interacts with true data through the signal of both biofeedback and neurofeedback, the information is accurately integrated into the specific area. This results in efficient, healthy, and happy outcomes. Daily life changes in sustainable highest quality of inner joy, psycho-emotional calm in front of challenge, and discernment to letting go entropic memories, dogmas and mandates of early childhood that ruin the 'taste' of personal life. Any obstacle dissolves to permit the dynamic dance of opening, by yourself, all the spectrum of your best evolution of human potentials.

The people of this humanity have worked on self-development for thousands of years. In the past much of that process has been colored by religious or social-cultural dogmas.

In this decade we have the capacity to create more effective inner change by honoring the wisdom traditions that work, and integrating technology that gives us real time feedback about whether the work we are doing is actually promoting real effective change. Modern science has proven that human brain plasticity can be improved with by short practices and with real presence in that here-now. The system is based in these scientific foundations and embraces a diverse range of daily 7-minute practices such as integrative movement, art creations, origami, tapping. The neurofeedback sessions, are usually 21 minutes of training for mathematical amplitude of specific brainwaves, at some locations only 14 minutes. This different style of learning makes a paramount difference in reaching fast results congruent with personal goals.

Story Telling – Wisdom Transmission

Around the world humans pass values, epic success, events with transcendent meaning, and pearls of wisdom by long or short stories. Most are shared in community locations at right time and place, such as during a winter storm with warm fire in a shared room. The imagination of each person was stimulated by the setting and community connection, and most stories were passed to the new generation from elders.

Modern life creates virtual reality, avatars, and instantaneous gratification, most in base to play games to kill, destroy, blow up others, and the result that is seeing in the youngers in the last decade is desensitization the orbital-frontal areas of empathy, and highest compassion. Discernment is blurry and bullying, violence, and justifications for wars has increased.

It is possible to have fun, enjoy journeys, share teamwork, and many others pleasure in this life beyond these violent computer games. Some elite that wants a society of slaves brainwashed coordinate this actual reality, however, the cosmic wisdom is a-temporal, and human physiology can be restored to self-freedom of healthy pathways.

Here one example, please used the story offered now, 'The Rat in the Dojo' in your next times of introspections, and connect the dots-information-pearls of wisdom with your daily issues, to reach an easy personal win-win-win outcomes:

"Once upon a time... ... in a place very far away, there lived a famous teacher of evolutionary wisdom, who understood his students and also the language of animals. One afternoon, a large and healthy rat showed up at his school communicating:

--"I have decided that this space is where I will be living from now on. I am letting you know, for your information." (1)

[1] This style of language is conceptualized in energetic formulas, such as clean energy 768, which meaning without chemicals of toxic origins, nor wrong potentials of psycho-emotional development. In the system this consensus learned during the inner work, allows clarity in the data evidential. From oriental wisdom meaning Chi Righteous plus Qi are circulating in the 12 meridians, in phi ratio proportion, with energy 96 (electromagnetism opens in the morphological field up to the second skin defined by the 8 extra meridians); and energy 48 (physical inner power also called cellular High Will / vitality, which is the energy that sweeps obstacles in personal life, when movements of power are executed with the self-discipline of constancy and inner quality). This palette of varied tasks nourishes, sustains, and promotes transformational changes in the physical matter. These concepts will be clear to you with reading the chapters that contain more information.

The master argued multiple sociocultural reasons why the rat was not welcome in that space. However, the animal spoke --"The arguments you express rest only in your personal reasons for living; they do not contemplate all the information I have given you. I reaffirm, I have decided that this space will be the one I will use to live from now on. To decide is to be free of fears, internal obstacles, and temporal inconsistencies."

The rat affirmation: "Here I am (Estoy), and I Am (Soy) a rat with the ability to exercise natural wisdom because I have truly worked with myself. My material and energetic form is just a garment that I offer to humans; but my pristine origin, like all in this universe, is in the cosmic forces."

And the rat entered the great martial arts practice chamber of the school, where it settled quietly and calmly. The teacher understood that this animal was an opportunity for his school and its participants to experience a new quality of perception. He chose to wait for sunset, when his students would arrive, to present them with this new situation.

A teacher of human evolution knows that Time is an appropriate dimension to perform evolutionary tasks, but only when information is consciously applied (energy 768), with psychophysiological tools (feedback, power movements, metaphorical and analogic practices), and considering the correct context (interacting both fields, the morphological and the structuring forms). It is then when that minute time of circumstance, event, and/or teaching, the information will be much better transmitted and easily integrated by the recipients.

After all the students had understood the reality of that "presence" in the other room, the master asked them what "efficient" suggestions they could offer for removing this rat from the school. The best student in evolutionary transformation practices for corporal matter spoke: "Let me personally take care of that rat. With the energies concentrated in my experiential axis, I will attack her without a truce, and soon the rat will be dead."

The teacher reminded the student that the intention was not to kill, but to get the rat out of the school and not allow it to return. The student entered the great room, closing the doors behind him. For some hours, sounds of struggle were heard, as were exclamations from the students. The night ended and at dawn, he left the room very hurt and terribly tired, without being able to fulfill his purpose. The master invited everyone to return at sunset and reflect on what had happened.

The master pondered: When we start a battle from the "I", the multiple personalities created by the education of the environment, and the "need" to show others success in competing and being victorious, usually are the worst enemies to face. To insist on using violence and on destroying the other is to create a perpetual chain of triumphs and losses, where fear is the underlying bodily chemistry. The instinctive mind wants to survive and feels threatened in its fundamental purpose for reasons that the intellectual mind understands and sustains.
Prolonging battles without discerning how much "battery" - "gasoline"- energy is still available, will push the physical body to exhaustion, illness, and

can facilitates accidents that can be self-destructive.

The teacher asked if anyone else had another attitude to deal with the school situation. An advanced student in the workings of body chemistry, neurotransmitters, transmutation of hormones, and emotional responses offered his point of view.

"Let me get into that room now, and before dawn, with my methods of releasing toxic attachments and adhesions, I'm going to get that rat out of this house. I will listen to its arguments and give it enough quality of options so that its personal fears and limits fade away and decides on another path in its existence. I have completed all academic instruction, plus I have the tools of ancient wisdom, to delve into the behavior, and lead those involved into healthier states."

The second student entered the big room and also closed the doors. All night you could hear some words being spoken and the sounds of psycho-energetic sweeps. With the first streaks of dawn, the student, in a total state of rational loss of himself, came out of the room and plunged into the river in an attempt to clean so much 'garbage' he had picked-up in his intention to be an efficient therapist healing psycho-emotional conflicts.

The teacher invited his students to return at twilight to discuss what had happened. When everyone was reunited again, they began to discuss the unaccomplished task. It is clear that this rat and its presence here is more than a simple task to face as a student at this evolutionary school, or, in a specialized personal therapeutic branch. Physical and mental challenges do not frighten this rat; and it accepts them as a primitive territorial struggle, and, with its inner power, observes the challenge without personal fear. It, therefore, persists and triumphs. Emotionally, having a clear discernment of what it wants to fulfill (to reside here), the rat can dismantle any perception of doubts, obstacles, and negative possibilities for itself that anyone tries to force upon her. Its answers are so coherent, logical, and full of appropriate terms, that the effort made by the therapist to try to "convince" the rat, modified the circulating chemistry in the personal circuit of the professional. All the while, the animal remains convinced that its reasons are valid, and its "right" to remain, inalienable.

The master asked if anyone else had any idea that night of how to eliminate that rat's presence in that room. An old student who always brightened up the classes and the parties with his "magic pranks" spoke:

"What the science of healing the physical body as a medical doctor, or killing him as a warrior, does not achieve, and, as we have seen, neither the efficient intervention of an expert in human emotions and the facets of the mind, perhaps my evasive tactics of deceiving the senses and their perceptions, of distorting reality with "magic" can achieve it. I am going into that room, and before dawn, the rat will walk away." He walked into the room and closed the doors.

Throughout the night there were intermittent noises, laughter, and silences. At dawn, the old student opened the doors and singing his song of madness, walked away. The rat, after greeting everyone from the doorstep of the salon with diligence and cordiality, closed the big doors and stayed quietly inside.

On the third night the students met with their teacher. Everyone was already overly concerned about the events, and wondered what could be done to solve something so complex. The master dialogued about the "value" of magic as an inner power to distract human attention, and to move the public's focus to more convenient points for the personal reasons of the magician. It allows him to carry out something considered impossible, and thus, impress everyone. That behavior is rooted in the inner need to be considered unique, incredibly superior, and the bearer of an extra human gift. However, those energies become toxic when there is a lack of echo in the receiver of the magic, thus reverting the effects on the person of origin. It is possible to observe the catastrophic prices that person "pays".

Developing human potential without previously having done the inner work of the cleaning of egos, obstacles, and temporal inconsistencies – living with extreme focus on the future or the past is a big mistake. Coherence between words, thoughts, and actions, (also known as living with integrity) is the best methodology of self-evolution. Those who live by lying, falsifying information, deforming evolutionary possibilities to obtain personal instant gratifications, never achieve the individual transmutation that opens the portals of cosmic forces.

Each student of this Dojo returned to their homes without having defined a plan to solve the circumstance. The river of life kept flowing and the rat still owned the martial arts salon, which did not leave the master happy. Later that year during a special sunset, a young student asked for permission to speak.
"I have observed the lessons that the presence of this rat has brought about in this school. I think this is an animal that has overcome its instinctive and

intellectual fear and, thus, deserves an opportunity since its clarity is beyond awareness. The rat's attitude is not one to harm the material person, nor to destroy the mind or energies of the one who opposes its decision, it only 'returns' as a truthful mirror, which is attempted to do to its animal garment.

"I know of an old female cat that lives in a neighboring village, she is highly appreciated for her essential wisdom. Perhaps consulting her could help the school achieve its goal. I suppose that to have the attitude of the caliber of admitting help from a "cosmic source" so far unknown, we all have to stop initiating the attempt from our own personal egos. Also, postpone individual reasons in order to focus on the global mission of evolving as "conscious principles of life" with the intent, beyond awareness.

<u>This quality of unconditionally, is required for to be the critical mass of change that irradiates cosmic evolution to humanity.</u> If we all agree, I am willing to travel to that town, find that cat, and ask her to please help us."

After all the students and the teacher too, deliberated on this proposal, they came to the coherent attitude of impeccable gratitude and humility of asking for external help to the lineage of the school.

The young man left at sunrise... After 3 days he returned to class and reported that he had found the old female cat. After he explained the situation, the feline promised him that, on the next full moon, she would come to the school. When that proper time arrived, at sunset, a healthy but incredibly old cat came to the gates of the school.

It showed nothing special, no armor, no sharp claws- only a serene presence, with high inner silence. She did not promise anything, nor did she explain what she would do... She just asked if everyone was sure that the rat should leave the martial arts room. With the total reaffirmation of all the members of the school, she then requested in detail:

- that nobody at the school do anything -physically, mentally or in any other way- no matter what happens that night;
- that each person be responsible and abstain from making any judgement about what they see happen;
- to not allow personal feelings interfere with the events that will occur;

- no claims or expectations based on individual points of view and appreciation;
- to maintain Inner Silence, and not open/bring questions to satisfy habitual thought forms;
- to only irradiate unconditionality into the Flow of the River of Life with total equanimity. [2]

[2] This style of language is conceptualized, in energetic formulas, as energy 12 dominant in the material, somatic cellular form; and energy 6 as an active complement to the cadence of fractals and bridges of the personal morphological field, which 'listen' to energy 3 from the 9 portals of the second skin the meaning, intensity and quality of information. It allows a dialogue between two life forms, without words.... Energy 768 was circulating in telepathic bits, with perfect and total clarity between them.

She curled up on a comfortable cushion that was given to her at the school. She closed her eyes but was evidently fully aware. All the members of the school were sitting in their cushions and maintained the meditative state that she had requested. Silence permeated the walls of that place. During some time, the cat stayed in that state of mindfulness, and her morphologic field was irradiating signals that only the rat, inside the other room, could perceive with total understanding.

The full moon advanced in the sky, illuminating the house, the garden, and the environment with pristine clarity. The old cat opened her eyes and, without making the slightest noise, opened the doors and left them slightly open.

A few minutes later, also without making any noise, she came out slowly and gracefully, carrying the rat in her mouth, alive and without harming it. She went to the garden where she got lost onto the horizon, in a direction where there were great mountains. Three days passed and, at dusk, the old female cat came back to the school. No sign of the rat in town.

The teacher and the members of the school received her delightfully and begged her to explain what had happened. "We were simply able to 'understand' each other, and we chose a win-win-win solution that involves shared success. That rat had surmounted its fears of everything, including cats, and had the inner power to know itself to be strong, capable of limits and boundaries that others never reached. Its discernment is clear and strong, but even the wisest being knows that there is an enemy that will always overcome us… natural old age, the final cycle of life. We are both elderly, and I proposed to her that she would be much more rested and happier if she, the rat, retreated to a space full of light, food, and warmth, without confrontations with anything or anyone.

There is a valley in those hills that is small but very warm and cozy, where the abundance of what is simple, but efficient, never lacks. I proposed taking her there that night, as it was very difficult for her to travel such a large distance because of her size; coupled with the unfamiliarity of the place, these were factors that did not allow her to recognize the advantage of that space.

Being a full moon night, we could travel more easily, and the rat, from my mouth, could observe the path with safety, learning how to return --if so decided-- after visiting that space of possibility for its destination of peaceful freedom. We did and, when we arrived, the rat loved the reality, the silence, the calm of not having to watch constantly for enemies- as she did in this room. We spent a day together and I then returned, since the rat decided that she was not interested in going back to this school, she is happier there… Its existence now has a healthy and happy old age.

Win-win-win solutions are winds of change that bring unknown but very efficient information, and that can only be integrated if the participant is encouraged to trust the impermanence, impeccability, and the unconditionality that life offers us, and is willing to test that 'opportunity.' The rat is happy and won't come back. You are happy to have the martial arts room open again. I will return to my village at the crack of dawn, and we will all be glad that we solved an unpleasant circumstance. It was the cooperative attitude that you all sustained during this process, without violence or anger, that made this outcome possible in the flow of the river of life. This is also in harmony with our mission statement: to create globally stable peace."

While the teacher and the students wanted to 'pay' the cat with money, food, and items - articles, she only accepted the pristine sentiment of gratitude offered by the students, with an open heart and silence of the mind.

One of them asked her if she could teach them how to be like her…

"To evolve is to initiate a long journey, and the best and most efficient route is coherence in what you think, what you say, and what you do every day.

Without this discipline practiced and integrated daily, we will only be navigating the waters of the river -at times, rowing against the current- pushing the future. But only when we understand the value of the unconditional acceptance of the here and now, as the impeccable moment to evolve NOW! It is that when evolutionary possibility shows itself to the fullest.

That person exists without procrastinating, delays, racing to be 'me first', and without priorities that are the product of a traditional education. It is: 'I AM in total awareness.' And there the original human nature manifests. There arises the capacity to radiate unconditionality and impeccability unto the flow of the river of life with total equanimity, thus, one of the highest possible individual evolutions expresses as a daily state of being. However, beyond my conduct and my inner work, there exists a more advanced teacher in a nearby village.

He is a very old cat. He is so efficient in his emission that, in appearance, it only sleeps in the main square of that village, next to the fountain of water. His impeccability is so high, that his presence in the cushion - made by the local residents so that he can curl up and purr-cheers up everyone. And when he closes his eyes, that subtle but very profound sound joins the sounds of the water. The liquid element cleans and nourishes that village, when it circulates carries the emissions of intention and/or the 'idea/form' that the wise cat sustains in its mental field, with an attitude of 'Doing Nothing'.

The pristine essence of its unconditional presence, impeccable, and in a complete state of equanimity, distributes the correct amount of information to the world of the rats, at the adequate place, and at the correct and necessary moment in time. It's a message of peace… there is space in the planet for the rats to be happy and free, but, in this village, the doors are closed, rats do not come in!"

> Liana Mattulich -- Adaptation from a Zen tale for this modern living space-time.

Living as a human in this planet is BEING an aware pristine state, with an atomic corporal form of emitting fields. Awareness is the capacity that humans have to decide what to emit. That could be a destructive ray that can scorch matter; it could be 'garbage' of toxic and violent thoughts; or… a gentle aromatic breeze of flowers and peace that nourishes the smiles of all living beings in the planet, and beyond…

Sleeping cat is the state of human evolution where the individual rests-meditates-builds-creates-manifests, from a cushion of timeless space.

There are tasks to accomplish individually during an incarnation, and many people accomplished their goals. When advanced masters sustain the awareness of unifying and joining, in a cosmic proportion, the interaction with other participants originates a subtle structure of cosmic forces called Buckyball. [3]

[3] Science discovered that carbon atoms have a valence of 4, and its properties are known. But multiple experiments have proven that the union of 60 carbon atoms, interconnected in a very unique geometric form, originates a different molecule called Buckyball, now capable of executing properties different from the capability of each atom individually… it is a cooperative mood what, a superconductor power, manifests. It is this new quality of terrestrial matter, elaborated by human intelligence, which is presently being used in various scientific fields.

The "beyond awareness" cooperative union of superfluid human beings in an energetic and coherent mental focus CAN manifest an intention/emission/idea-form on a global scale. They can attempt planetary peace for all living forms in the solar and galactic system.

The very well-known phrase from Master Masons, "as is above, is below", is valid here. Modern technologies like the Geneva particle accelerator in Europe have shown great similarity between the quantic dimension of subatomic particles, photons/electrons, and the configuration of the elements of the human body and the planet.

The images from space, obtained from scientific telescopes, show similarity between the space-time web of the universe and the microscopic view of the topographic cellular distribution of the brain and cerebellum. The physiology of the human energies and forces fields are harmonic when both have been worked through one self-regulate integral evolution.

Transcending words and the integration of our senses in an interactive lattice are the ideal tools when humans intend to manifest their best quality of life. By the emission of dynamic abstract images with Colors, Aromas, Textures, and Universal Sounds (CATS) the spectrum of pristine principles of cosmic evolution transmitted high information. Pythagoras spoke about the music of the spheres, the opportunity when dancing lights and forces. IT IS in this synesthetic data possible to engage the Key of the creative pulse of the fabric of the universal cosmos.

Some years / cycles ago I knew was the perfect timing to start my last chapter of teaching as a master operating from energy 6, to humans who had already done the inner work to receive what I had to offer.

Life allowed me to share a story. 'The Rat in the Dojo,' is about a female Cat that knows win-win-win outcomes. You were able to enjoy that stories a few pages ago. Here now we are going add another layer on how to connect dots – fragments of information to form meaningful connections.

As the story explained, because the young student was capable of thinking beyond rules, dogma and daily habits, he explored the idea of meeting the sleeping cat and learning from him.

With courage, the student travels to the unknown, and when he arrives, the sleeping cat welcomes him. It is a relationship without words ….. Transmissions of the essence of cosmic wisdom start to happen.

Cut wood / carry water, the Zen approach to enlightenment of inner silence in daily life, plus passing of time, the hair color of the young human master changes to white. He becomes 'present' when people from the town, with pure heart and happy eco, bring small 'details' to him and to the sleeping cat, just in the exact event which, these things, will help new wisdom manifestation to benefit the entire space-time of that dimension.

The human master learned unconditional presence … and when the cord of time was singing, the old sleeping cat becoming sparkling stars with aromas and laughs, a free form dancing happy wellbeing in cosmic dimensions.

A new quality of sleeping cat form closed its/him eyes in the fountain of water. The teaching of becoming from student-sage-human capable of thinking out of the rules and daily habits, to explorer the new Land of Forces was transmitted.

This is OUR reality in this cord of right time. I am, such as the sleeping cat, <u>learning how to learn</u> beyond psychophysiology of matters-bodies; chemistry-emotions-energies; and fields-mathematical alchemy-vivencias; to the possibility of transcending to Forces of Wisdom of BE … SOY-ESTOY --- Beyond Awareness, Land of the psychophysiology of Forces - - -   teamwork…….

The internet opens perceptions beyond the older style of one to one, and we can share and enjoy stories, practices, sounds, events, etc., and ….. Without narrow frontiers, in open field of perceptions ….. by dream-work.

Humanity is only one of the owners of the future on this planet.

Together we 'win-win-win' dynamic balance of self-sufficient living in harmonic states of peaceful health with inner joy.

Individual goals accomplished by self-regulate psychophysiology, can being intertwining in success with broad joyful environmental forms of life, -animals, plants, crystals, plus scientific technology. Together as teamwork we can join Free states of sustainable wellbeing.

From stories to a foundational orientation of synthesis of wisdom of science and spirit using technology, we will share some of the practices; such as some metaphors that are integral to changing your "circuits" to live with greater health, joy and freedom. As we mentioned at the beginning of this book – CHANGE requires intention and action.

Metaphors and Sensory Integration

Axis- the Axis is a paradox in the context of linear thinking because it has a very complex energetic physiology—with multiple roles.

Now is the time to start building your personal Axis:

Get comfortable, be still, and become aware of your body and your breath. Go deep within yourself, allowing soft and gentle breathing to expand your belly.

Relax your shoulders, allowing your jaw to hang. Your eyes can be softly closed or looking down, without focusing your mind on anything in particular.

Feel your feet on the floor and relax them. Feel the energy and warmth flowing through your body calmly, but firmly have the sensation of being there.

You are in contact with the earth; this is our home, and it is nourishing you. The energy of the earth is growing in you, and it is giving peace and silence to your mind.

Now you are ready to sustain calm, deep breathing, focusing your attention on that part of your physical body called your backbone. Perceive each bone; notice how, by working together, they are the artifices of this miracle that is you, capable of moving, walking, swimming ... so many wonderful tasks that you are able to do. Say 'thank you' to them. Also perceive warmth; there is plenty of blood circulating, alive and very strong.

What kinds of secrets do these bones have? Every bone is articulate; thank your flexible disks. They work in harmony, as a team helping each other. Together they make you flexible, efficient, safe, and happy.

Feeling the healthy relationships inside of you allows an emotion of joyful self-acceptance. Yes, your physical body is a living system of parts that work as a team, not in competition. They know the rule of inner natural wisdom: "win-win-win." Helping each other makes life easy and healthy.

Sensory Integration - Synesthesia

Some people are born with Synesthesia, which is like a physiological wiring of the nervous system that allows the senses to make internal connections between all the sensory areas of the brain; remarkable people, such as artists, musicians, etc., have used successfully in their lives. However, the new neuronal pathways developed by HIKE training allow the multiple sense perceptions to happen in synchronicity, calls it 'Sensory Integration,' or SI. Order in what is used is a fundamental methodology. 'CATS' is a word that helped inner work. C -color; A -aroma; T -taste/texture; S -sound. Using all the senses is an interrelated journey that enhances the internal connections in and among different areas of the brain-body. Perceiving the taste of a color, the sound of a texture, the aroma of music—all these are synesthetic physiological links.

It is this higher, integrative function of the senses that is capable of interfacing with the physical body, and it is that informational interface which really works! It is by combining thoughts and sensory perceptions simultaneously that we can access the inner nature of healthy balance, and the reception of more subtle messages.

Awareness assignment to integrate the senses in building your Axis with Sensory Integration:

- Emphasis is placed on experiencing joy, because this creates balance among the neurotransmitters responsible for communication in the nervous system.
- Apply CATS; C back to front; A front to back; T up to down; S left to right.
- These are the <u>self-heal pathways</u> most efficient.
- See your favorite color(s).
- Remember things that make you feel happy.
- Find the most gorgeous aroma that really energizes you - smell that.
- Bring the memory of a taste that you enjoy (maybe delicate or strong) – taste that.
- Discover the texture of joy beyond any limits – touch that.
- Hear and encompass all these with music that makes your spirit soar.

Acknowledge that symbols and signs can be "seen" differently on occasions of dissimilar moments. Be creative and put away judgment based on old culture-time structures.

Safe Place

Building a fantastically safe place is a very old technique of the ancient wisdom teachings. It allows one to reach an inner point of dynamic balance and presence, while overcoming the distresses of externally difficult environments. This unique space contains the entire spectrum of what you want. It also has four doors, one in each cardinal point (North, South, East and West) that in other levels of the teaching we will learn where and why they are connected. Request that your body equalize both hands at the same warm temperature. Center yourself in your Axis. Allow your legs to root deeply into the core of the land.

Safe place is not located outside of self; it is not related to time or space. No person or thing can touch that center. It is yours alone. There is no right or wrong in this space. All the best that can possibly be imagined is found there – creativity, inner joy, and the full expression of your senses, which are the tools for building this inner reality.

Positive memories, like a sanctuary in nature, provide the sensation of being in a safe place, which allows calm, self-acceptance and loving feelings which support self-growth. This experience is enriched with sensing deep inner meanings through multi-sensory information.

It is a perfect space, A-dimensional, A-temporal. At this level you can understand that this is the door between dimensions (your personal singularity). Only from this key point in us are we capable, with humor, to accomplish the "impossible mission" of going "where no one has gone before..." the unknown, and success!

Letting Go in Symbols

Many people feel there are things inside of themselves that they don't like or that give them an ugly feeling. For you to move beyond this attitude, find an animal, bird, or other symbol of whatever you consider unpleasant. This symbolization should represent aspects you would like to let go of.

Memories of long term, and internally repressed events, create an energy drain which steals our vitality. This results in clouds and fog that distort our perceptions. Use of personally selected archetypal forms (symbols) help liberate even intense suffering.

Don't give high credence to the symbols that will emerge while doing this work. They may come as a flash and relate to the origin of the issue, but the source is not primordial or related to the essence of who you are.

Symbols are tools that your unconscious mind uses to "let go of" repressed materials. Give up your intention to analyze deeply. The ideal, efficient attitude is playful acceptance and forgiveness.

Imagine these internal feelings transforming into your chosen symbol, and perceive them crawling, falling, flying, or shooting out of you. Your breath can aid in dislodging by blowing or coughing. If the symbol is like a snake, you can let it crawl out of your feet, or a bird can fly out of your hands or your head, like a thought.

Be sure to send it far enough away so that it goes well beyond your second - energy skin. Take a few deep breaths to thank yourself for identifying and releasing old uncomfortable or painful experiences or memories. Fill yourself with warmth regard and inner joy. You are free.

Backpack – Mountain Journey

Allow yourself to go inside your Axis – the warmth, flexible pathway filled with light.

You are embarking on an adventure carrying a backpack, and you resolve to scale a mountain. During this process, be creative and imaginative, utilizing all of your senses. As you start off, take note of the colors, the sounds, the fragrances, the tastes, the feelings, the shapes, and textures surrounding you. Walk along enjoying this environment. You come upon an inviting granite rock and decide to climb on top of it to rest for a while.

Sit down with your backpack in front of you and begin to unpack. Enjoy the vista. You choose to throw away any heavy or unnecessary items that you have been carrying on your shoulders.

Allow your unconscious mind to use symbolic forms to also release itself from its unwanted burdens; for example, a rock that smells like a rotten apple.

Become aware and open, let go of your feelings attached to each object. Say out loud what you are holding and your first impression as what it represents. Release the object and follow it with your eyes until it disappears from sight. Any residual feelings that were associated with it, goes with it.

Deeply feel thanks and extend appreciation toward these things that have served you well by guiding you to where you are today. Their departure opens up space and lightens the load, making it easier to carry your pack.

You continue on this upward spiraling path and release any other items when you feel so inclined. Upon reaching the summit, look around and appreciate where you are, using all of the five senses. Perceive this new freshness and thoroughly enjoy your sense of freedom in this peak experience. Take some time to fill any voids created with soft, warmth regard, and self-acceptance.

Backpack – River Walk

You are walking with your backpack in a special place, aware of all the sensory stimuli – notice the colors, the sounds, the fragrances, the tastes, the feelings, the shapes, and textures. You come upon a wondrous river. You sit beside it and liberate more belongings from deep within your backpack.

When you are ready, resume traveling on the path along the river.
You can encounter some friendly animals. Dialogue, observe and enjoy them; each one has a message for you.

You come upon a stranger and decide to share with him/her a portion of the food or possessions that you still have in your backpack.

Be thankful for being able to freely give to another, as well as holding respect for the articles you have left. Enjoy the perceptions of becoming a transformed, mobile, resilient being – lighter - with a song emanating from the marrow of your bones.

Journey with Water

Go into your Axis. From its depths, come to your safe place. Relax there. Now you are ready to open the south door of your safe place and journey to a beautiful waterfall.

It is important to maintain the feeling of granting freedom to all of the forms you encounter in this journey, which may include archetypes, symbols, people, and emotional patterns and thoughts.

Now, observe the richness of your environment, the entire spectrum of colors, fragrances, flavors, sounds, feelings, vibrations, shapes, and textures. Perceive the freshness and movement of all the elements in their various forms – Wood, Fire, Earth, Rocks, Air, and Water.

Absorb yourself in this special natural place and experience flowing through different expressions of water. Sit by a lake on a sunny day observing the waves. Play in the rain. Watch a rainbow in the sky after a storm. Dive under the water and feel the sun streaming down through it. Float on the water during hot weather. Paddle over the waterfall and let it shower over you, giving away all the pressures and dirty aspects of yourself. Perceive the wholesomeness of you, totally clean, free, and healthy.

Flow with the river and go into a deep crevasse. Note all the forms of life, small fishes, vegetables, their colors, sounds, textures, tastes, and odors. Here you can play with the beautiful fish and other aquatic life, including plants and rocks.
Return to the surface with joy and thanksgiving emanating from your heart,

your blood, your immune response, and energetic structures.

Green Meadow with Large Balloon

From the center of your safe place, go and open the south door. There is a beautiful path, safe, and full of light. Start walking in this warm winding path, be aware of every step, using all of your sensory perceptions of this very special place -the colors, the sounds, the fragrances, the tastes, emotions, the shapes, and textures. You pass between two trees and enter a big green meadow.

A group of your friends have come upon a large balloon. The hatch is open, and they are putting all of their saddest memories and symbols of past problems into it -anything that has ever bothered them. They invite you to join in this — "gifts of liberation." You select a number of things to let go of in that way. Take care and look deeply inside for things that really disturb you, cause stress in your body, or, suck away your life energy.

After everyone has released their burdens, together all of you disconnect the cords that sustain attachment to the balloon. If so desired, do the sweeping exercise one or three times.

The balloon departs rising into the infinite sky and disappears forever in the stars. You and your friends, who represent the various roles that you have assumed (in this human life or past lives), decide to go home. Come back to your safe place more at ease, thankful and full of joy. All of these together are You, your Axis. These are your best integrating aspects. Please enjoy them!

Hand Warming Metaphor

This session introduces the "inner key" of warming both hands at the same time, increasing their temperatures to the same degree. Mastery is reaching 96° F or more, in less than three to five minutes, and sustaining this temperature for ten minutes. A difference of 0.5° between the two is significant. A decrease of 0.3° F throughout the session is considered a normal fluctuation for the average person. The environmental temperature needs to be comfortable. Please make yourself at ease in terms of releasing muscle tension and adjusting your clothing, your position in the chair (table), blankets and pillows used, the amount of light, volume of music, and the feedback tones, if you are working with thermal feedback computers.

Warming and balancing your hands is one of the most important modalities for reducing distress, addictive behaviors, thought patterns, and cravings. Outside of feedback sessions, start paying attention to your body's temperature. Your hands are paramount.

Keeping them warm has beneficial effects in the deep hypothalamic centers of the brain, which regulate body temperature, water balance, appetite, gastrointestinal activity, sexual activity, and emotions.

Biofeedback generally uses two thermals on the fingers, one in each hand. In addition, electro dermal response (EDR) can be used on the left hand for women and the right hand for men. When it is used, electroencephalograph (EEG) sensors are positioned at various locations on the head. The "thinking" conscious mind is not the main actor. Autonomic/automatic network mind is directed toward maintaining the thresholds of the neurofeedback-EEG. The feedback sound makes learning easy for the brain and nervous system, and it is improved by sustained positive reinforcement.

Direct your attention to metaphor and the development of your inner key by the synesthetic ability to stimulate all the senses at once. In these practices, you will learn to generate feelings of inner joy and maintain a sense of awe at the wonder and magnificence of the world. Joyful emotions create a better balance in the production of your "feel-good" neurotransmitters and contribute to physical and mental health.

Ideas for Warming Hands

The metaphors used in the HIKE system allow you to build a perfect inner space safe, loved, and free of worry, and/or any concepts that are disturbing you in reaching inner peace. To warm your hands play with nice memories.
It can be a wonderful sunny beach with warm sand, the top of a mountain with the sun warming you, a gorgeous house - monastery with nice fireplace, the warmth of the arms and skin of your loved one… allowing yourself to blend with that space, the feeling of warm peace, inner silence, and total self-acceptance.

Your heart will be in resonance with your deep breath and your physical body will start to relax deeply every fiber, every cell… bring the best opening to your arteries and see the blood circulate freely, warm, and peaceful, a healthy flow of nutrients and oxygen to your capillaries, making your skin warmth, giving deep inner peace into all aspects of yourself.

Immune System Metaphor

Stimulate meridian points in the Water element with acupressure, tapping, or sounds by tuning forks or bowls are a good complement in this practice.

Remember to center yourself in your Axis, be creative in the healer aspect of self. Utilize your best intention to reinforce, recall, and activate this experience with positive realistic images. The immune system needs factual information that is true to life.

See these healing cells flowing, circulating, and penetrating all tissues in need of healing. Give each of the specialized immune cells their own personality using all your skills of sensory integration.

You may want to perceive macrophages as cells having a big mouth; antibodies as soldiers with effective magnets that attach to the enemy; killer cells that eat any mutant cells, such as cancer; and bone marrow and thymus as the generators of new healthy cells. Remember the membrane-skin of the cells is the ideal place to add a healthy signal—as the 'mark' of aware self-regulation decisions (a flag, a flower connects in the membrane of the cell). You are healing yourself by your inner power.

"Warm" is life, which gives to the new cells the symbolic signal to be healthy, efficient, happy in a warm environment, and that is you!

These images, symbols, forms, and shapes interact in Golden Mean Proportions that will improve physiology and the sense of well-being. Golden Mean Proportions are mathematical relationships of harmony in life forms.
Symbols and signs can be "seen" differently on occasions of dissimilar moments. Be creative and put away judgment based on old culture-time structures.

> **"By defining and defending the self, the immune system makes life possible; malfunction causes illness and death. Study of this system provides a unifying view of biology."**
>
> -Sir Gustav J.V. Nossal, MD

Analogies-Symbols

Axis is a metaphor for words expression, but integration in daily life it is a personal symbol that embraces the essence of self.

Some analogies are roots in common sense approaches, others in scientific data, however, all of them are creations individualized by the sensory integration of the CATS quality of selections done; they are giving the opportunity to call 'Inner Keys' because open perceptions in self to new horizons of broad possibilities, in a never lasting evolution.

Four legs correlations are among planetary elements, locations of the cranial meridian points used to train with neurofeedback, and dominant purposes, which are there working efficiently. The structure of this energetic formation (two pyramid opposites correlates in dynamic cadence of Torus dance) is one of the foundations of the psychophysiology of human fields.

> **Frontal leg** --- Fire, Discernment – Clarity – Creation – F3 (left)
> **Right leg** --- Water or Air – Cleaner Space/Time - F4 (right)
> **Tail** --- Earth – Ground – Cleaner – Inner Silence - P4
> **Left leg** --- Air or Water – Observer – Manifestation - P3

Sounds

Hearing nature's voices is a privilege rare today for most people that are living in big cities. Anyway, by records of real events, it is possible to use these gifts as nourishment of own internal reality.

The two journeys of Voyager, provided us with sounds from our solar system, and are now sharing more information from our galaxy. NASA sold copies of these solar system recordings. Spending 21 minutes of neurofeedback training immersed in the crystal music of the Rings of Uranus, Saturn, etc., are vivencias (life affirming events here-now without previous memories to check) that effectively transform the alchemy inner work in a personal tasteful joy. The cosmos vibrates in mathematical resonance with our cells, molecules, and atoms. The 'music of the spheres' named by Pythagoras, opens our personal perceptions beyond awareness dancing inside the field of forces.

The languages of some animals are also interesting experiences for people to cross the small field of the cognitive consciousness to the big land of beyond awareness. Explore new possibilities, wood sounds and plants speak in signals that galvanic response measure and are used in some research to know the truth, because they never lie, distort and/or cancel a data.

Art, Reading, and other Creative Acts

The Arts in Human Inner Keys for Evolution system includes several modes of creative expression that integrate, modulate and extend the changes in the psychophysiology achieved through all feedback technologies and practices. These modalities are critical to the evolution approach, because they evoke the Pristine Program's natural resonance with the Phi Ratio harmonies and balances, allowing the students to embody the new quality of life. Phi ratio is a universal relationship, easily seen in physical proportions on the human body, nature and universe. Marine shell, sunflowers, clusters of stars, pinecone to name a few. When a line with any length is divided into two unequal parts, and the proportionate relationship of the small segment to the large is the same proportion as the relationship of the large part to the whole line, we have a Phi ratio --mathematical term. This is called Golden Mean in art and in ancient wisdom.

- *Drawing and Painting* increase one's discernment in connecting abstract thought with colors and two-dimensional forms.
- *Collages and Moribanas* integrate multiple free-form elements into a coherent balanced representation of a meaningful concept.
- *Sculptures encourage* the creation of 3-dimensional forms in Phi Ratio using diverse materials, from nature and/or recycling circumstances.
- *Origami and Zen Garden* transform two/three dimensional designs into harmonious, meaningful creations which build fine tune motility, and inner peace.
- *Tonal and Musical* expressions are used to evoke synesthesia and the chemistry of inner joy, self-acceptance and self-gratitude.

Reading

HIKE system encourages people to read a broad range of materials from the medical, quantum physics, astronomical, and ancient wisdom literatures --before, and after training sessions. These materials help participants:
- Reevaluate the 'rules' imposed by cultural education and/or family;

- Remove counterproductive patterns of thought, feelings and behaviors;
- Restore the natural capacities to enjoy and be in the self-Pristine Program;
- Renovate their perspectives on life's possibilities beyond previous limiting ideas.

Journal

Human Inner Keys for Evolution System encourages a private journal, where every training of feedback is registered, to maintain a personal relate of the progress, and also, the practices and experiences that come during the vast palette of techniques learned.

Creative Acts – Connection with Awe-Wonder

It is important that we recognize the value of expressing ourselves and experiencing Awe in spaces beyond words. This can happen with

- Music – creation or enjoyment
- Math
- Sports – movement
- Time in nature – under the sky, with a tree
- Connection with animals

"Nothing in current science can account for consciousness, yet consciousness is the one thing we cannot deny. The exploration of this final frontier has now become imperative. Now, more than ever, we need to understand our own minds, and our sentience, so that we can achieve our true inner potential." -- Peter Russell

"Our scientific power has outrun our spiritual power. We have guided missiles and misguided men." -- Martin Luther King, Jr.

"Whoever said that a small group of concerned, committed individuals cannot change the world? In fact, it is the only thing that ever has." -- Margaret Mead

CHAPTER TWO

Technology of Neuro / Biofeedback in Human Inner Keys for Evolution

Feedback machines act as a scientific mirror/map that allows humans to gain expertise and quickly master effective self-regulation of inner states according to his/her personal pathways and goals. The participants are working with a screen of phone or computer, which with the precise objective physiological data in real time allows an effective communication between one's mind, and their autonomic nervous system.

By using powerful metaphors that have been used for thousands of years in the world's spiritual traditions, people engage their intellectual mind, while the neurofeedback screen is presenting audio-signals to the physiology of the body. The metaphor sustains the mind's focus while the feedback signal creates an electro, chemical, 'internal state' new loop of well-being.

Using the "distracting effect" of the wisdom tools allows one's "automatic somatic pilot" to register the dominant frequency that is received through feedback, and to enhance the frequency's amplitude / strength (millivolts). This is probably one reason why it is difficult at first for students to verbalize exactly what has changed inside of them. Nonetheless, everyone recognizes changes within themselves and others.

Self-regulation used with this kind of inner work style, bypasses the only cognitive consciousness. It is stablished in the healthy domain of the physiology, which learning very fast in this scientific way. This quality of learning to learn (ancient wisdom helped by modern feedback technology), helps sustain daily life with a new more efficient metabolic somatic flow.

The HIKE system offers a unique style of combining biofeedback and neurofeedback.

Methodology of Neuro and Biofeedback Sessions

During the first 2-3 minutes of feedback from the machine, the participant internally verbalizes the goal she/he intends to achieve. With eyes closed, or very quiet, the participant focuses on an appropriate metaphor, while allowing the body to learn the physiological work by means of the audio signal of the feedback machine.

During the last three minutes of training, people will call for the emotion of gratitude "from you... thanks to you."

Immediately after the session, and before sharing with someone else, the person should write down what they experienced in a journal. This helps integrate as an active memory, the pathways used in the session.

The thresholds utilized during brainwave training, in the feedback system that HIKE uses, are set from the scientific software in specific mathematic correlation to a phi ratio proportion seen in healthy life. This only happens in units designed for our use. Our system promotes optimal performance / opens human high potentials, which allows the participant to choose inner freedom to change, self-heal, and transform personal life.

Common feedback machines are made for healing different ailments, dysfunctionalities, and/or illness, may not respond in the same way.

Neurofeedback (NF) in this system rewards the participants 85% – 90% of the time when they enhance the amplitude of a frequency selected above the set threshold, using distinctive sounds as feedback signals. Self-training in your house is a modern luxury possible that allows you freedom, supported by the soft virtual guide of the masters of HIKE4Evolution.

Principal Training Sites in the HIKE4evolution system

Site	Location	Primordial Function (according to HIKE)	Frequencies Trained Hertz
Cz	Central line, between the front of two ears	Coordinator of body-minds-electromagnetic field-soul-spirit	↑12-16
Czp	2 finger widths posterior of Cz	Immune system door	↑7-11
F3	Left frontal	Discernment-creativity	↑23-25 or ↑40-45
F4	Right frontal	Let go	↑7-11
P3	Left parietal	Power of manifestation	↑40-45
P4	Right parietal	Silence in mind	↑6-8 or RAW

The brain as the central organ of the nervous system is one of the more complex mysteries of modern science.

During NF training the brain is building connections among different quality of cells: The neurons most commonly known are the neurons responsible for voluntary movements and sensory-perceptions. These cells function with alternate electric current – brainwaves- and chemical neurotransmitters. There are also frontal mirror neurons for empathy and executive functions; and just some years ago was discovered a collection of nerve cells called claustrum's-conscience neurons, that appear to be responsible of switching cognitive states.

Human's brain also contains glia cells that function by direct electric potentials. Glias are called the 'whispers of life.' In Germany glia-cell-feedback is used to define the presence of 'Awareness, or, Will' in people, who are in deep and long states of coma.

The central and peripheral nervous system work in collaboration with cerebellum, membranes-meninges, spinal fluid, sympathetic and parasympathetic cells, etc. The entire nervous system offers multiple electro-chemical pathways and preferential zones for diverse tasks.

We will intend to understand in simple common-sense words how brainwaves contain and transmit information. Let's start with some basic science.

It takes a photon eight minutes to travel from the sun to earth. When it arrives on the planet, and travels to the back of the human eye, it interacts with the retina and one chemical enzyme called 'rhodopsin'. Rhodopsin takes the energy of the photon and turns it into a pulse of alternate electric current that travels through the ocular nerve, crosses the optic chiasma and lands in the occipital areas of both hemispheres where the perception of 'seeing' happens. Recognition and other intellectual functions are possible by a memory bank, and very complex processes of energies-matter-conscience.

The electric frequencies that the central brain produces are measured in Hertz and the amplitude of those frequencies is described in millivolts. In people without inner work most have brain wave frequencies of low voltages --- less than 1 millivolt to 3 millivolts. With training in NF for self-regulation it is common to measure 3 to 7 or more millivolts. Many advanced masters registered 20 millivolts and more in special states of high awareness. (Called by ancient wisdom schools: illumination-enlightenment).

At the beginning of last century, brainwaves were shown to be the result of 'real' electric current in the nervous system. Due to limits of technology ---on those years was inefficient to report so low voltage -- the medical doctor who discovered that data, decided to cluster four groups of frequencies together. The names for these groups of frequencies are: bands 1 to 4 Hz delta; 4 to 8 Hz theta; 8 to 12 Hz alpha; 12 to 16 Hz beta. Despite the development of more advanced technology, these old naming / traditions are difficult to erase in the field of professionals, as well as the general public.

<u>First Foundational Concept</u>: All individual brainwave frequencies, described as Hertz, have "different" actions, based on location and amplitude. The same frequency of brainwaves at different locations may have different effects.
For neurofeedback training, in this system, we use 3 to 5 bands of consecutive frequencies --- at specific locations. (Ideally these are locations that are both standard neurofeedback locations as well as cranial meridian points). These protocols are given with specific tasks related to the location of the sensor, and

with the 'intent' to duplicate the amplitude that was registered, at that place, at the time of the baseline of the starting session of the learning curve.

This style of working allows the natural interaction of glias which are nested in the region, plus the energetic blend of righteous Chi-Qi-and/or Ki at the healthy meridian circulation. This methodology seems to facilitate fast learning and integration at psycho-physiological dimensions.

In the last 50 years of inner working with human beings who have the 'intention' to self-evolve, I saw a commonality: when the amplitude of the brainwave voltage is doubled compared to the values seen at the beginning of training, the brain wave changes are associated with other behavior changes. Those people, shows a new inner power. The older style of baseline chemistry and electrical patterns associated with the old 'mood' of the unconscious mind, plus the neurotransmitters that were habitual reactions to daily events, both are now modified ... This new quality of chemistry is present at High Will, -inner power / force developed by the exercises. It is sustained during times of need and circumstances.

Second Foundational Concept: Specific neurofeedback locations on the scalp of the head are used, during training, to reinforce specific brainwave frequencies. They are individualizing based on the persons goals and natural predisposition. For example: Cz is a cranial point with different intertwined actions at the dimensions of the physical human form, and in the realms of energetic spaces. Neurofeedback point's locations overlap cranial meridian points. We combine intentions / inputs for synergistic results.

From the biologically – western point of view, Cz is the cranial point located at the top- midline portion of the head. It is over the part of the brain where the neural fibers create a bridge that is responsible for the communications between brain hemispheres.

From the energetically – eastern point of view Cz is the area of the central meridian where, the 12 rivers of Chi of the physical body, are engaging with the cadence of the 8 extra-meridians, which structure the morphologic human field of peripheral energies. Also, Cz is the realm / cosmic space location of oriental ancient wisdom of the cranial chakra of light-enlightens.

In general, most people showed in this location window-bands of brainwaves between 11 to 18 Hertz. When they training to duplicate the amplitude of their personal frequencies, they obtained inner power to self-regulate and create an inner state of a grounded, centered, calmness. It is important to note though, that within the wide spectrum of 11-18 Hz frequencies, 70 to 75% of humans easily work self-regulation and self-healing within the band of 12-16 Hz; a minority have their bands oscillating in a slightly different range. For example, between 11-14 Hz, are used by participants that have artistic sensitive tendencies. The system suggested 13-15 Hz to people that are easily distracted and need extra support to be able to sustain focus. We are seeing the frequencies around 15-18 Hz as dominant in modern people, who have the habit of multitasking. They 'suffer' from never having enough time to apply and sustain serious inner work.

Brain plasticity is one area of optimal human functioning, which creating and manifesting, enough personal flexibility in seeing different options-pathways-self healing.

When they use the fuel of 'High-Will,' which is developed by the movements of inner power, they create a better self-chosen outcome.

Participants with optimal brain plasticity showed resilient behavior to recover quickly from stresses that arise in their personal life, from environmental circumstances, and global chaos.

For healthy brain plasticity to occur,

NEVER train the human brain at the same band in all the areas.

Those mistakes of the times of 50-60 decades of past century, and/or modern sound system of 100-104 Hz binaural beats, made many people damaged and destroyed their future high potential possibilities. Healthier brains and nervous system in harmony with immune responses, and psycho-physiological functioning, are like dynamic dancers in a symphony, where each brainwave is one instrument of the concert, which together 'intent' to make the natural music of the cosmos.

The Human Inner Keys for Evolution system works with neuronal brainwave frequencies at 9 to 11 cranial locations: Cz, Czp, O1, O2, F3, F4, P3, P4, C3, C4, Fz. These points are slightly modified from the rules of traditional NF methodology; really these are areas in the scalp with the 'presence' of meridian activity with fields of different energies. The participants train to learn and recognize by personal finger sensory perceptions these areas, and are guided during the learning time by Masters of the system. Here the awareness and 'intention' of the Master in service - that acts as guide with wisdom tips- is paramount. They have the purpose to always respect the goal of the participant.

<u>Third Foundational Concept:</u> Learning to learn and practice self-evolution to heal a personal life, requires applying 'intention' during the training time by using analogies, metaphors, and stories, etc. This methodology keeps the intellectual mind busy in synesthetic pathways, with psycho-emotional value in the personal goal of life.
This style of learning to learn allows the automatic mind to utilize the scientific data from the signals of feedback system, without the distraction of input by older habits, and/or inner dialoging of the untrained monkey mind.

Our system has registered, in the form of manuals, interactive games, and spirals of evolution, the entire spectrum of tools and practices in progressive order to provide necessary building blocks to implement self-evolution. Information in sequence applied at specific training locations and with right timing, is the 'key factor' of the fast results of the system, plus the expertise of the Master trainer, which allows for healthy outcomes in the participants by guiding them on individualize specific important details.

<u>Fourth Foundational Concept:</u> Fast integration in all of the dimensions of human being with sustainability will happen based on the practice of the movements of inner power, audio-visual data of scientific information, and homework.

These additional materials help to transform the psychophysiology into a soil with good nutrients, where new ideas and inner powers, such as 'High-Will' are developed and stored in right places.
Daily time investment is short but requires consistency. The average commitment is 7 to 15 minutes daily, with the precise details which empower the movements, breathing synchronization, and focused thoughts.

To learn this system is to open personal perceptions of a multifaceted crystal. For many practitioners make common sense, in the way that the dots are connected, by ideas and information that are always cooperating in win-win-win outcomes. From that point of the practices, the personal life flows as a serene river. Evolution, as we affirmed before, is applying cosmic order in daily life.

From seeds that germinate in nutrient soil in good weather, to mathematic proportions in the structure of any form that 'intend' to deliver a perception of beauty and harmony, life in this planet is a process of right location, right information, and right timing dancing simultaneously.

The right locations to apply sensors of NF and to develop easily fast self-evolution are 9 to 11 specific locations called cranial meridian points. Also, we use about 12 additional self-tapping locations in specific places on the body — related to the quality of 'intention' in the session of training with brainwaves. The right information of the materials offered in order guides the mental focus of the NF training. The data is read before sitting in the computers. In most cases the participant with closed eyes internalizes multi-sensory visualization during the 21 minutes of NF self-regulation training.

The right timing is the proportion of daily life that the participants focalize in their inner work, (average 7 minutes of practice per day), with the consistency and commitment to make the most of their 'intention' to build new open self-perceptions with healthy and efficient results.

When people learn to use all the opportunities that daily life provides to practice awareness and self-regulation of psychophysiology, the old paradigm inoculated by the family, cultural, and social education loses importance. The authentic real Being / Essence executes the birthright to BE all that you want to be, with inner freedom and joy.

"You have the right to change your mind" was the motto of one of the pioneer companies of NF in past decades. Self-healing is a fast pathway to achieve a new quality of life, sustainable in freedom forever. Right here and now do a personal experiment.

> Please, take a deep breath,
> Focus your thoughts on a beautiful color…
> Makes the perception of one aroma…
> *Enjoy* that…

We will intent to analyze 'why' we do this practice as first space-time shared. *Breathing* is a 'physiological nutrition' more important than food and drink. Just a few minutes without oxygen in lungs, cells and tissues, and the matter form dies.

When people breathe, most of them are unaware of the process, all that is happening with each inhale and exhale. Each breath creates complex dynamic physiological changes of the nervous system (both electrical and chemical), exchange of molecules, pressure of gases in lungs, blood, tissues, etc. That absence of self-awareness, during breathing, is reinforced by education that always looks outside for more input, combined with pressures from the socio-culture, where never time is enough to do basic self-care tasks.

Being aware and choosing to change your thoughts is a birthright, which modifies personal life in healthy states of well-being.

Joy is a simple but deep pathway that is infrequently used by many people. It is a force that exists independent of external circumstances. The practice of self-gratitude creates a chemistry that circulates in your physical body, resonates and is stored in your energetic fields. Self-Gratitude is a powerful self-transformative tool that increases your capacity to experience joy.

With each breath we suggest focusing your thoughts on a Color and then Aroma, which is the perfect sequence-order in the synesthetic pathways, fast physiological avenues that communication back to front, and front to back for the human nervous system.

Human beings connecting with true biological information facilitates self-integration; that 'order with proportions' in the process of learning creates brain plasticity that opens perceptions beyond awareness.

In addition to the scientific information of biofeedback and neurofeedback training, the Human Inner Keys for Evolution provides data about order and proportion in other ways for learning self-transformation. Metaphors, analogies, stories and integrative movement are 'languages' used in traditional wisdom to share information that is difficult to express in common words, and/or too complex for be absorbed easily. The Human Inner Keys for Evolution system includes these additional forms to the modern wisdom science to support people's capacity to cultivate their "inner power."

One of the first and foundational practices is **GROUNDING** – by a variety of methods. **Axis, CATTSK, Three Legs.**

Grounding yourself by using analogies:

Axis as pathway of encounters all the 'realities' that each human is by birthright, and education distorted in inaccurate narrow small frames.

The active building of creating a coherent personal Axis is done by application of intentional synesthesia, breathe power and heart variability.

The mnemonic CATTSK- sensory processing is one specific order:

- Color
- Aroma
- Taste / Texture
- Sound
- Kinesthesia

This facilitates the natural flow of inner neuronal avenues of physiological data, which is individualizing in each human being as unique person in this planet.

The exact correlations of personal color-aroma-taste-sound-and kinesthetic vibration of inner and extra skin fields are information accurate as DNA, tone of voice, fingerprint, and iris map.

The next grounding teaching is Three-Legs, as analogic 'tail' from the coccyx area, which connects the matter reality of the human body with the core of the planet. Humans learn by that communication respect for all forms of life in this blue gem, plus recognizing the capacity of clean ourselves in active attitude, receive nourishment and support for daily life, and cooperate to create a better habitat for all.

Changing Biochemistry by Changing Physiology

The next obstacle that humans have in their 'intention' for self-healing in their personal life is to change the chemistry of our old habits.

Reduce the inner power of stress created by a hormonal-chemical response is a difficult task for most people. Using biofeedback to help retrain your autonomic nervous system response provides you with greater resilience in everyday life.

Using thermal sensors to increase your finger tip temperature and decrease your skin electro-dermal response is an important part of cultivating inner power, or the ability not to be a slave to changes in personal chemistry. These two biofeedback tools are foundational for quickly obtaining a more stable mind-body condition and are some of the best antidotes to psycho-emotional distress.

In parallel is common to apply a methodology for help discernment, by clarify the difference between personal desire, --a product of the education and habitat- from real need, -- what is required for life- and focus with clear mind in what really want as goal in which to invest the personal 'intention.'

At the beginning when the system is used, during a session of NF, techniques for letting go are applied during the feedback training, plus symbolic imagery to reinforce the inner work, and complementary movements to release stuck-issues that were pressuring the personal life of the participant.

How long does this take? It all depends on the attitude of the student, commitment shown, roles of victim and/or superheroes, in most cases, without enough real energy to have success.

These are the times where "new physiological pathways" are building in the totality of the student. The processes are empowered by very efficient tools. Are daily reminders to sustain presence with awareness, called Tools for Awareness. The entire spectrum of the methodology is taught in simultaneity. When done in cadence with heart rate resonance, it creates synchronicity in the personal energetic morphologic field.

The sequence of learning includes;

First know yourself by creating your Axis with your individual CATS information.

Second clean the garbage that you've accumulated during life, but without forgetting to nourish yourself and recharge better quality of energies in self, by the practices of movements.

Third is integration and integrity. Integrate what you are learning into daily life. Making new habits to be healthier and efficient starts when your own thoughts, speech, and actions are implementing with consistent coherence, at every moment possible.

When these three aspects are applied, the knowing of your personal Safe Place engages new information and experiences that will facilitate discover-training-execute efficiently other aspects of self. The legs start to connect with planetary elements, becoming 4 legs, and each pyramidal form overlaps at that Safe Place intra-corporal giving clarity in the discernment of different qualities of energies. Added concepts of doors with meaning-purpose and helpers in Safe Place, transform that location in a real unit alive of the aware new potentials, called singularity.

The knowledge of quality of energies and their specific reality in the planetary spectrum allow new dimensionalities to life, second skin, morphologic field and the field of forces that structure the totality.

The constant flow on the meridians becomes for many humans in toroidal circulation.
The scientific data that now is daily information in the life of participants, makes them connect the dots and 'see' with open perceptions the simultaneity between planetary electromagnetic field and second skin; also, they can correlate the gravitational center of the forces of nature with the High-Will stored in humans' bellies. These levels of practice open our inner capacities to listen --from a deep point of self the symphony of vibrational notes-Inner Sound, which body-minds-fields emission together.

In this step during neurofeedback training the Cz cranial meridian point, opens a new function in the psychophysiology, now is capable as 'director of the orchestra' to individualize the 4 areas on the head which are called antennas. Through training, a new structure develops in people. There are two energetic pyramids, one pointing to earth another pointing to sky. The apices of the pyramids – intersect in your safe place. This structure promotes the circulation of the energies, elements, and self-intention creates and manifests at right time-place this geometric pathway of light and self-evolution.

From these steps, continuing to refine our inner work is possible. This depends on individual background, specific goals in life, and environmental situations.

Observer

The physical body that humans wear is a powerful complex structure, where multiple and simultaneous processes happen constantly. Metabolism intertwines proteins at many places, cells, organs, and three forms of electricity — alternate at neuronal circuits, direct potentials in glias and skin, electromagnetism in cerebellum balance, etc., play daily life. Immune responses, hormonal cycles and a myriad of molecular, microtubules resonances, mitochondria's discharges, and subatomic processes are all woven together.

The physiology of the body also works with diverse energies, such as heat, ATP, and the toroidal electric field of heart. The immune system combines the hormonal-chemistry-cellular responses to environmental circumstances and engages with all the spectrum of planetary energies —For example:

Solar flares and cosmic rays from supernovas create mutations in human DNA; barometric changes trigger migraines; lunar phases influence planetary and body liquids, such as menstrual cycles, oceanic tides, to name few examples. All the spectrum of energies natural and manmade —cellphones, TV, radio frequencies, etc., are interacting with the matter-body form constantly. All in this known world is connected, and in some mathematical proportion intertwined.

The methodology of Human Inner Keys for evolution is not linear, because nothing in human life can be seen only in one narrow way. Adding your commitment to self-awareness makes the journey to live from your true nature more efficient. With this kind of inner work, you really transform into who you want to be. That is powerful self-healing!

To apply science to our 'aware intent' is engaging the innate cells of the creative pristine program that evolves in the human race as in everything in this universe. That blueprint is universal and shows mathematical relationships. Our own human position as 'observer' of the outcome has the possibility to define win-win-win potentials, by reorganizing our fields and harmonizing personal life to the global goals of this humanity, evolving in inner peace and communitarian progress.

"Socrates said that if people know what they should do, they will do; but he underestimated people's ability to fail themselves. Everyone knows what they should do, but how many people actually do it?" -Tsai Chih Chung

"The human brain is an enchanted loom where millions of flashing shuttles weave a dissolving pattern, though never an abiding one, a shifting harmony of sub-patterns. It is as if the Milky Way entered upon some cosmic dance." -Sir Charles Sherrington

CHAPTER THREE

Eastern Wisdom, Points and Bridges in the Morphologic Field

At this moment in the teaching, it is evident that human bodies are complex interactive systems that accomplish many personal and social goals through the strategies developed by the intellectual mind. However, without knowing enough about the internal connections in the psychophysiology, the basic plan that nature gives to all life forms: be healthy, efficient and happy, is destroyed in many people by the urgent 'needs' to have success, in terms of the socio-cultural rules of space-time where they are living.

Understanding the functionality of the heart beyond pumping blood, and recognizing that it has a strong electromagnetic field which influences the frontal and orbital portion of our brain, and that there is more information traveling from the heart to the brain than from the brain to the heart, clarifies their relationship. The linear western education, way of thinking of past century, does not honor this truth.

In some cultures, meridian points and the management of Chi flows is studied, and mastered by many medical doctors. The western' societies requirement 'scientific proof' and, this validation has been done. A few years ago, the University of Peking at China, defined the spectrum of Chi-energy in the range after infrared and before microwaves. From that research Western medicine started to consider this field as an alternative in health care.

Eastern Medicine in Modern Times

New technology has allowed us to learn more about our structure and function, and gives us the capacity to integrate more of the wisdom from Eastern health science. With the information provided by electron-microscopy we learn about intracellular microtubules. Plus magneto-resonance helps us to see how dynamic many of our physiologic processes are. Now, nanotechnology, gives a new dimension to our investigations, research and treatments. Where there were once obscure concepts, now we have a greater understanding of deeper realities in the human body. Modern science is more integrative, looking at immune responses, hormones behaviors, and the quantum field. All this makes evident the necessity of teamwork among scientists, because nobody can open all the doors of the psychophysiology through self-centered speculations.

Meridians, Extra Meridians, Assembler Points, Attractor Area

Now it is known that meridian points are the rivers - channels of a quality of Chi-energy with the properties that can modify, with correct treatment, the quantity of the Chi flow and also, refines the quality of that band of universal energy. When that transformational training is accomplished, the eight extra-meridians start shining and reinforce the natural boundaries of the electro-magnetic field that humans have. That is similar to the energetic cocoon of the planet, also with dynamic toroidal dance, which is protecting life forms from harmful solar explosions and cosmic rays.

In their interactive role with the central nervous system, meridian points are doors that can be used in neurofeedback treatments simultaneous to the training sessions, to engage quickly the learning plasticity of human brains. Integration of meridian points in the NF training shortens the time and effort required to obtain excellent results. Older traditions and fears of the unknown paralyzed the integration of these useful treatment additions for many long years.

As meridian points now are considered viable therapeutic options for most chronic diseases and supportive elements in optimal performance training for the inner work of evolution, these so called 'assembler points' are now to be recognized and used. These are specific areas in the physical body which can be utilized to rapidly modify, the mathematic proportions in the quality of human energy. However, the most important role of assembler points is being bridges among the bodies that humans develop while working on their own evolution. These bridges used at the right time and place allow universal pristine forces to be incorporated, engaged, and embraced in human form. Most of these areas are defined by three points that bring easily, in the human perception, the memory of triangles and also, the geometric form of tetrahedron pristine pyramid in these locations.

Nine zones are paramount for the inner work of self-evolution. The keys to open some of these areas were maintained as a big secret in ancient wisdom schools, and sages did not discover some of the correlations and synchronized pathways without spending long years of self-research. Those areas showed dynamic catalytic effects in the state of awareness.

In the zone of the shoulders, a triangle is formed that Zen meditators hit with the wood-stick intent on opening awareness. Shamanic schools used hit this zone with the wrist; the highest master impacts the psycho-chemistry state in that body, and by that, modifies the level of awareness in the practitioner (example: Don Juan techniques with Castaneda).

In the base of the nose, where the septum finishes in the upper lip, is another point that helps support efficient store of memory information and better recollection of data.

On the sides of the head, in the parietal-temporal zones, are the locations where the energetic cranial wings emerge after doing inner work. The wings have a geometric form that corresponds to three cranial points in a triangle tetrahedron pyramidal configuration.

The Human Inner Keys for Evolution system teaches coordinates and correlates the areas of the wings with psychophysiological achievement, but only after enough inner power is collected by the movements done during a committed time.

People who have done the inner work of 'Higg Will transmutation', are able to experience 'vivencias' to reach sustainable states of "beyond awareness," without the use of psychedelic substances.

For example, the meridian points of the gallbladder channels, are activated through internal work focused on self-evolution within the system. The gallbladder channels are located on both sides of the body—in the frontal-orbital areas and the parietal-temporal regions and in wisdom traditions and sacred art are called the four antennas or horns.

By combining the knowledge of quantum physics with human anatomy, individuals who have engaged in the internal work of transmuting what I call in English Higg Will—or Willpower of high quality—can experience deep states of being/awarenss and attain stable levels beyond simple cognitive awareness. Higg refers to the surname of the American scientist and Nobel Prize winner who discovered the particle known as the Boson—Holly Grey-Higg Boson. Peter Higg waited 50 years for his mathematical discovery to be validated by the particle accelerator in Geneva. Sometimes, science lags in quantitative proof of what ancient wisdom has shown for hundreds of years. If you wish to investigate further, look into the Neuroscience Laboratory, Department of Psychology, and the Keck Laboratory for Functional Imaging and Behavior at the University of Wisconsin, USA. In August 2004, they presented brain maps of monks from the Shechen Monastery in Kathmandu, Nepal, which were validated by Princeton University. These maps demonstrated that meditators with over 40 years of self-regulation training in their minds showed high amplitudes in gamma brainwaves across four areas of the brain – aka the "antennae" regions.

National Geographic, one of the world's leading magazines, featured on one of its covers the face of the monk who agreed to be the "lab rat." I honor here his great compassion and agape love for humanity.

While serving as President of the Association for Applied Psychophysiology and Biofeedback (AAPB) in Colorado, USA, in 1998, I presented the brain map of an advanced master within my system who had activated and stabilized those zones (the 4 antennas) after only nine months of inner work combined with specialized neurofeedback practice.

Of course, the local professional community assumed the EEG recording "had" to be an artifact, since no one had ever shown results. They also dismissed the data because my medical degree was "only" from Argentina (With focus on other ways of being of service, I chose not to repeat credentialling in the United States.)

With time others, duplicated the results that I had obtained with self and others. It is now accepted that inner work -produces stainable, reproducible high voltage gamma waves. These brain wave findings are no longer interpreted to be artifact or seizure activity. With the integration of science and technology, ability to access this state of consciousness is obtainable by people who don't have 30 years to hang out in a monastery.

Moving on to other applications of this integrative approach.
On the inner and outer sides of our ankles, there are important meridians and energy points. On the inner side, four finger-widths above the tip of the ankle and behind the tibia, there is a hollow. This is where three energy channels intersect. On the outer ankle, also four finger-widths above, lies another significant energy point. This is the area where the "ankle wings" emerge— another symbol attempting to correlate the human potential of inner work with universal forces.

Meridian points of the bilateral frontal orbital areas, and also, at the Gallbladder meridian of both parieto-temporal zones (called five antennas-horns) are opened with this quality of inner work of self-evolution in the system.
Combining the knowledge of quantum physics with human anatomy, people with 'Higg Will transmutation' inner work done, are able to experience 'vivencias' to reach sustainable states of beyond awareness.

On the inside and outside of our ankles are important meridians and points. On the inside, four personal fingers up from the tip of the ankle bone, behind the tibia is an indentation. In this area three energy channels intersect. On the outside of the ankle bone, also up four personal fingers, is another important energy point. This is the area of the emergence of wings, another symbol that corresponds to the human potential of inner work with universal forces.

These inner and outer points around the ankle have specific uses in the battle for freedom of the human singularity from gravitational force. Dancers in classic and modern styles have discovered sometimes that the pressure at the big toe (special shoes in classic school of dance) give an equilibrium, a burst to make the impossible possible… they support graceful movements that seem like flying, levitation, out of the law of gravity on this planet.

The areas called 'hearts on the legs' – just discovered by science a few years ago but valued in 'secret' wisdom schools, synchronize simultaneity wing powers with heart rate resonance and breathing techniques. This self-observation practice helped by High Will power collected with movements, and distilled as elixirs, are paramount for develop harmony among body-mind-energies-fields-forces. It took seven to twelve years to reach success in ancient times, and today the modern scientific technology of biofeedback makes it easy to learn this in few weeks.

Second Skin, Bridges at the Morphologic Field, Portals

The system affirmation: Meridians are the doors where is possible to modify the rivers of Chi energy in the physical body, to reach healthy quality of life. However, there is one additional concept-dot to connect and understanding our energy anatomy.

Righteous Chi is the quality of Chi energy that in many schools is called Vitality, because is proportionally resonant with the Force of Life. When there is a daily practice of metabolizing Righteous Chi, it gets distilled and fuels vitality and evolution at a deeper level. Within the system – the daily working with Righteous Chi includes filling three cups and renovating their chemistries, moving those energies through the twelve body-meridians and eight extra-meridians. These energetic structures clearly define the morphologic field, as space-cocoon of the matter form.

- Dantiem Self-Gratitude;
- Third Eye Self-Acceptance;
- Thymus Self-Love;

When these layers of inner work are accomplished, the Pristine Program of Self-Evolution totally activates the Assembler points, and new efficient behaviors start to show up naturally, because the untrained intellectual "monkey" mind, -by the practices has been tamed and transformed into a "Pet-Mind."

This new evolve quality is capable of cooperation in awareness without the heaviness of dogmatic structures, which before guiding the outcomes. Discernment in the frontal area of our brain is activated by the NF training in the areas called antennas.

The simultaneity of the system allows confluent 'moments' – right timing specific in each sage, where the conditions of electric pathways, neurotransmitter in different dominant formula, and the process of healthy and efficient inner work is done. Then perceptions open easily in a new domain.

When energy 24 (See the energy discussion in chapter 4.) is dominant daily in the morphologic field formula, the book of cosmic information consistently opens for that person on the right page. The external signal for this connection is the original smile… Now vitality connects the Force of Life, and awareness connects the Force of Light-Information, plus the personal cadence is engaging by the Force of Movement, which it is supported by the consistent practice of the exercises beyond the NF sessions.

Assembler points flourish with this work, and bridges start to be built among these doors on the physical skin, and on the surface of the second skin, these locations are called portals. These new pathways, brain plasticity-pliability and quality of phi ratio relationship on energies formulas, are given subtle improvement in the participant.

If the movements of power are accomplished in vivencias with nice adaptation to this growing process, Axis, Dantian, solar plexus, and other zones manifest self-transformation, and become Attractor point-line-form… Ancient wisdom had a lot of symbols in sacred geometry that correlates with Attractor zones integrated in matter form.

Dancing impermanence is here the daily aware choose target, nothing can be done ritually; all is a new unique discovery personal opportunity and, with perfect 'Inner Key' conditions. Forces are intertwined in daily metabolic physiology, and Force of Evolution opens the individual subject to the possibility of becoming, by Self-High Will, a new member of a Buckyball group.

The layers of the system have an *order* to connect the dots, correlate the information and manifest the Observer.

The guides of masters of human evolution are open to recognize opportunities to jump dimensions by suggesting the right time-place to practice the self-awareness intentions. However, suggestions are never imposed, marked as dogma any data, practice, and/or training, because the system always respects the natural individuality and free will of each person.

Tapping in the System of Human Inner Keys for Evolution

Tapping is listening to yourself. It is a technique that is used in ancient wisdom for millenniums… However, now, it is taking scientific validation by research done in many different cultures and places of this planet. It is an easy topic to study/practice, as homework.

Obtaining efficient results depends on several factors: location, quality of rhythm, strong grade of the pressure or hitting the area, and time in what this technique is applied.

Specific characteristics of individual participants, such as quality and proportions of energies in the morphologic field can modify cadence in the rhythm, deepness in the process and other details. As a general indication: only the personal 'echo' of your hands with 'intention' to hear, plus apply the most nourishment self-healing attitude, will make the difference between a simple routine of hitting specific locations, or 'really' transforming that place into a healthy melody, truly happy, and efficient for yourself.

Tapping YOURSELF is an easy way to integrate all the corporal-matter reality, plus the subtle bridges of energies in evolution around you.

Those new formations called fractals / bridges are in the space between second skin and the external skin-dermic cells barrier. That location around physical human body is called morphologic field.

General concepts for using different fingers for tapping.
These concepts never are 'written in stone':

- Index finger is proportional in action more at the mental forces;
- Medium large finger is proportional in action major at circulation, heart and emotions as chemistry;
- Ring finger is proportional in action mayor at sexuality, as force of transformation with hormones' metabolism;
- Small finger is proportional in action major at immune response and predispose to balance body-minds, and allowing toxic personalities dissipated.
- Thumbs always are forces in action and are ideally for applying pressure techniques to the deepness grade that is some uncomforted –with some degree of pain when initiate the practice. Maintain the pressure ---soft rotation can be applied- to the time that all local discomfort is gone.
-

The tapping rhythms suggested below are soft guide from ancient wisdom, and your best 'passport' always is listening to yourself!

Cadence is your personal, unique way, to BE in dynamic balance with your realities physical, plus beyond awareness, atomic structures, electric frequencies, particles in fields, etc. It is your speed in life where all the aspect that you are, as past, now, and future, are dancing in harmonic proportion of self-evolution.

It is a difficult concept to grasp, however, evolution is a cadence of cosmic life, and entropy is the chaos of waves lacking respect for others.

Nobody is equal to others... similar yes, identical... never... Be open to accept: if your changes are real and developed new evolutions in your life, the map used before... will not be an efficient instrument now.

I explained: Beyond Awareness is.... the unknown! Discovery is a daily 'Journey' to enjoy and learn constantly.

To evolve is to understand that all in this universe is impermanence, and to maintain rigid practices because they are written, taught by a guru, and/or prescribed by sociocultural traditions, narrows your new possibilities. Self-discipline to accomplish enough experiences is paramount factor in success. Also, is very important open discernment, to discover the right time to initiate a new practice. Wisdom is to know when to let go the contents of the back pack, however, High Wisdom is to know when to throw away the back pack, and move-on with self-freedom in safe pathways.

Tapping and Acupressure Points to Practice:

Basic location for ground yourself (feet in energy 96) and empower your immune response is: **4 gates**. These are four acupressure points found on your feet and hands.

Start with your feet, applying pressure with a specific chosen finger in the space between the big toe and the second toe. Use your left hand to apply pressure to the right foot. Massage from distal to proximal moving up a couple inches until you reach the end of soft tissue. Cross your left hand to right foot, to the space outside the right big toe. Then repeat on the other side, right hand to left foot.

Next, focus on the area between your thumb and index finger. Use the thumb of left hand to massage the area on the right hand, or vice versa first. If start by left thumb connects the line between the two phalanges of that thumb with the soft skin of the place on the right hand. Push --with intention- the first phalange of the thumb to the position that is direct up to pressure down at the hand; it is seeing as 'hand pushing' is in maximum extension up in the air. It is in the reception area one small hole in the tissues --in most people with some degree of pain. Opening this point is a healthy routine always before any session of neurofeedback.

Also this is a good exercise to do first thing in the morning. Massage your 4 gates before starting the normal activity of that day. Be centered in the best energy of the planet and 'inform' your immune system that you are ready to initiate another day it is an act of self-respect, which people forget a lot in modern life.

Another important area for self-massage is the area around the forehead and eyes. Make a triangle with your fingers. Place the thumb and middle finger in the middle corner of each eye and the index finger in zone of third eye/middle of the forehead. Sustain this position for 3 to 7 breathes with eyes closed. It is an easy technique to help let go from all the busy minds from the socio-cultural rush that we were immersed in, before to sitting in the chair for training. This practice predisposes the body-mind to do better deeper inner work.

When chemistries are agitated, the midline line between the upper lip and the nose is in general painful but, with soft pressure is possible to make that signal of discomfort go away, and a new calm state will integrate new possibilities. Review your 10 best memories during this breathing tool, and applied your intellectual mind in the quality mood of healthy Pet-Mind cooperation.
Both ear lobules can be massaged circular, pull soft and twisted in gentle ways; are there a lot of good points that calling calm in the psychophysiological realm of humans; this wisdom pearl-tip is ignored for most of the people that destroy those areas in many ways. The ancient forms of Buddha's are with evident longed ear lobules, as visual 'proves' of their inner peace.
Tapping the thymus gland is one important reminder of how the hormonal human evolution must be guided to really change the wrong habits imposed from socio-cultural and educational ways. The best location is the central chest in the line that intersection the horizontal line defines by both nipples, when they are in normal places. With age or lactation gravity pulls the nipples down.

A common rhythm for tapping the sternum over the thymus is 4-3-4 with fast one of the series. You can tap using 3 fingers, or some people prefer circular movement in that area.
Sustain these practices during the next time of development and growth and your self-regulation to evolve through your goals will be reached fast and with plenty success.

Here I am sharing another story to help you enjoy your journey.

"If You Know How to Breathe, You Know Eternity"

Many centuries ago a pilgrim was walking in the Himalayan Mountains in search of the "Lost Truth." It was twilight and the sparkling stars foretold the chilly hours in ahead. In the gathering darkness this honest wanderer noticed a formation in the nearby rocks and, looking more closely, he discovered a small, but comfortable cave. Once inside, however, he immediately noticed an elderly sage sitting silently in meditation.

With the clear intention of not disturbing the ancient man, he was thinking:

> 'I am younger, and I can endure the cold weather outside,
> rather than interrupt a Master in his inner work.'

Nonetheless, the kindness of his thought was heard by the sage, and he opened his eyes and said:
"You are welcome inside here. Please, come in."
After a moment the ancient moved deeper into the cave and came back with two hot cups of Tibetan tea – a mixture of herbs with yak butter that's high in nutrition and especially tasteful to people in that cold land – and he offered one to the younger man. They sat in silence for some time, the only sound to be heard was the howling wind outside foretelling the storm that would soon be upon them.

> "When did you leave your home?" asked the ancient.
> "Seven years ago," answered the younger man.
> "And what do you seek on your journey?" he asked next.
> "I am looking for the 'Lost Truth,'" the wanderer replied.
> "However, it's not in the high monasteries. There I learned only discipline and mantras.
> And it's also, not in some seekers that I've encountered on my way.
> Although each has pieces of the truth, each of them was convinced that 'his piece' was the most important."

The younger man sat in silence for a moment, and then continued:

> "I've walked in jungles, I've crossed rivers, and I've climbed mountains – in both good and bad weather. However, no place seems to have the 'Lost Truth.'
> I am sad and tired; and last night I began to wonder whether it might not be better to let go of this lifetime and start my quest again in another physical body. It's evident that my karma doesn't allow me to reach my goal."

The young man's sadness was genuine, as was the sincerity in his heart, and this the sage observed with eyes that shone powerfully in the soft darkness of the cave, as if they were gems of fire. He drank his tea slowly while reflecting on what he had just heard.

"Karma is a relative truth," the Master eventually said.

The younger man was totally focusing on the words, with his heart, mind and chest all directed toward the ancient one. And, in a sign of great humility, he knelt down on the floor and said:

> "Please, Master, have compassion on a young donkey like me who wants to know such High Wisdom. The fire in my chest is so intense that it doesn't allow my breath to flow. I think I will die without knowing my essential purpose, and I
> only want to live if it's by a real truth."

After considering the earnestness of his plea, the sage spoke these words:

> "Life is a school where each of us comes to learn some piece of the universal wisdom during a particular incarnation on earth. How well we learn gives us a quality of energy that travels through our cycles of re-birth. It can be shining and sparkling energy, such as you bring with you here today; or it can be a dark, heavy energetic vibration.
> Everything that exists is energy, and every energy in all its possibleform is needed -for the universe be what it is.

Then he added:

> "Karma is simply the backpack we bring into each lifetime from previous ones. Because it is on our back, we don't pay much attention to it.
>
> Nonetheless, it's a motivator that moves us toward our 'desires' – the arrows that take energy from us that enable us to grasp something outside of ourselves, which we ultimately come to realize is never 'enough.' However, if you're a real seeker, at some timely moment you will stop and begin to earnestly look within – occupying an internal space of self-observation. It may take a while, but you'll begin to notice that you're wearing a backpack. When that happens, you can bring it in front and open it.
>
> You'll discover all kinds of things in there – maybe some heavy rocks, oranimals that you had enslaved, or other entities feeling the sadness of having been closed in there for so long."

> "Moreover, now that you know what your pack contains, you're free (If you have sufficient compassion and gratitude) to let go of any object or form of life that has been in there, simply because you no longer need it. And, in fact, you'll also be free in that moment to experience the deep joy of discarding the backpack itself – and with it, 'karma' as well. 'Karma' and the contents of the backpack aren't really YOU, they're simply the things you've been unconsciously carrying around . . .
>
> for ages! You'll now be a new, freeman, reborn to your true nature!"

The eyes of the younger man filled with tears of joy, and with his face beaming he said:

> "Thank you Master, you have made me a free man!"

During the long silence which followed, the stars that had earlier been covered by storm clouds again began to shine in a symphony of notes and colors. Then the ancient spoke again:

> "Humans have this beautiful dress: the physical body. Nonetheless, they look outside of themselves for tools,

teachings, and 'secret information' in order to progress and evolve. And, worst of all, is when people engage their intellectual minds in a search for 'Lost Truth.'"

This last comment left the younger man stunned, and he opened his awareness as never before to capture every nuance of what he was being told, as the sage continued:

"The mind is a wonderful gift that we possess on this planet. It helps us in so many aspects of life, but it's never the means for obtaining inner awareness because intellectual information does not align with the 'pristine program of wisdom' that the physical body innately contains. Our living systems of cells are remarkable. They work like teams and automatically maintain our Essence in this physical planetary space. The physical body possesses a level of 'the highest wisdom' that the mind can never reach.

"However, because the mind speaks in words and humans use them as a bridge to communicate, they focus entirely on the language of words and forget to listen to the body. When we focus ourselves on this inner reality — by asking how our cells, in working together, are able to make us healthy, successful, and happy — it is astonishing the complexity and wisdom that each cell, and each network of cells, has within it."

"Well, how can I start listening to my body more carefully, Master?" the younger pilgrim asked.

"Everything is by 'doors,'" the Master replied. The body is an energetic space within which universal wisdom resides, and when we give our attention to its different doors, life starts to function on an inner path: one solid axis similar to your backbone. There new areas open, and our expanded qualities of perception begin to enrich, engage, and evolve us. As a consequence, we develop highly attuned bridges of real harmony among our realms, or dimensions, of functioning."

As the waves of wind outside the cave sang against the silence of the night, the ancient said:

> "One of the first doors is our mouth. What do we eat, and how do we eat it? And with what kind of awareness? The answers to all three change our chemical responses and our metabolic capacity to absorb nutrients. If you eat junk or dirty food, you're not respecting your inner space, and you create toxic conditions within yourself. Or if you eat with your mind filled with violence, struggling with dark thoughts, and/or filled with noise and chatter – and you don't savor the smell, texture, colors, and the enjoyment of eating – you're not taking in the 'nutrients' potential effect and only passing food through you. That's not really nourishing yourself."

He then took a moment to formulate the next key point, before saying:

> "The next doors are your 'Let Go' doors, and both are connected to your digestion. The first is your kidneys. When it's respected, there's illness because the kidneys are the reservoirs of vital energy. If your water is full of toxic components, the kidney door can't possibly maintain the 'inner lake of your belly' in a healthy state."

As the common sense of the Master's words begin to forge an understanding in the young pilgrim, the older man continued:

> "The second Let Go door is your intestines, and when food is stuck there, it's because the fire needed to metabolically process what you eat has been seriously weakened.
> Why? Because your cells are working in a non-synchronous rhythm with your cycle of life. Learning your cycles and living according to them allows your body to internalize and activate its pristine program of wisdom,' and to adjust your daily evolution to that. However, if your mind pretends to know best and to tell the body what to do, this innate wisdom is overridden and we end up ill and at odds with ourselves."

> "But the most important door of all – the one that really opens all the bridges and, consequently, all communication within

and between our ever-evolving capacities, is in our nostrils. So think for a moment about how we breathe. A group of cells in the deep primitive part of our brain create a reflex circuit. If oxygen in our blood is low, we inhale deeply, to satisfy that 'need.' And what happens when the carbon dioxide in our blood builds up? This unconscious 'miracle process' – governed by a group of cells that are not part of our 'conscious' mind – takes over, andwe exhale it."

"This what babies automatically do, and no one teaches them the conventional ways of breathing. In fact, they breathe in a way that virtually all of us adults have forgotten and, therefore, ignore – especially when they cry!

Have you noticed, my young friend, that when babies cry, they empty their lungs of carbon dioxide completely?

Yes, they seem to exhale every molecule of air in their lungs as they shout out with the only voice they have – and only then, when they have expelled all of the 'bad' air in their lungs, do they bring in a fresh supply of oxygen. That is their 'inner wisdom' operating.

Most of us have allowed our minds and our cultural experiences to teach us to ignore it. So, pay attention to this fundamental truth, and ask yourself:

'How long are my exhales?' Are they as long as your inhales? Well, my young friend, to breathe in a healthy way we need longer exhales than inhales! Why? Because your customary process usually doesn't fully empty your lungs of the toxicities and energetic blocks that have accumulated there. Your mind is thinking: 'Hurry up and inhale, or I'll die;' but your pristine program knows the opposite – 'Fully exhale the negative things in your lungs or you will die!'"

"What's the lesson for you, young man, as you support your life through breathing? If you breathe by reflex, life passes quickly. But if you breathe with full awareness, eternity exists within you! Therefore, knowing how to breathe is the most powerful door that our human physiology possesses to promote rapid evolution, with life proceeding joyously and successfully. But because we are culturally educated to pay little attention to breathing, we think that breathing practices are boring and a waste of time – something that we just don't need. And so life passes and passes . . . again and again."

"So please remember, my friend, that your breath is the unique KEY that opens ALL the doors to a healthy, fulfilling life. And, 'Yes,' as you have now correctly guessed, 'IT is the Lost Truth' that you have been seeking, and it's been within you all this time!"

Liana Mattulich -- Adaptation from a Zen tale for this modern living space-time.

CHAPTER FOUR

Recognition of Energies Useful for Self-Regulation, Self-Healing, and Self-Evolution. Enneagram as a Universal MAP

Basic concepts

It is a birthright be free of make questions, and develop behaviors different from the habitat, but without physical violence, and/or abusing others at levels psychological, emotional, economic, politic, sexual, etc.

Innovations, imagining new things that were never known before, and applying this innovation for the benefit of yourself and community helps create a better quality of life for all planetary forms, and it is one of the aspects of human evolution.

Scientifically, we know that matter and energy are aspects of the same original nature and can be interchanged (Einstein's equation $E = mc2$). Tangible matter is made up of planetary elements and represents a denser field than the field of energies.

The periodic table of elements is a scientifically accepted map. By measuring the number of protons in the nucleus of atoms, we define the name and position of each element; they are then organized based on the energy of their outermost peripheral electron. Hydrogen is the first element in the table and has been assigned the atomic valence of 1 (its energetic capacity to bond with others). For example: water is H_2O because the oxygen atom has a valence of 2—meaning it needs two hydrogen atoms in order to form a water molecule. In the realm of energy, waves are organized according to their vibrational speed. The spectrum ranges from low frequencies, such as radio waves, microwaves, and infrared, to higher ones like visible light, X-rays, and cosmic gamma rays. Becoming familiar with this dimensional reality of the human experience is an intriguing inner path of expanded perception. From elements to energies to the forces of quantum physics, science units our human experience from macro to micro. All is united in the universe.

In the realm of energy, waves are organized by their vibrational speed. The spectrum ranges from low frequency like radio to microwave to infrared to visible light, which we can see with our eyes, to X-rays and Gamma- cosmic rays.

In the story of this humanity were times where advanced ideas were studied, researched, conserved and recuperated for next generations by writing about, without distorting their cosmic values and common sense. Lao Tzu, and other oriental masters, plus the Persian/Arabic people created abstract ideas, formulas, and perceptions most in astronomy and mathematic, to help learning wisdoms, and proportions at their time reality.

From these traditional wisdom foundations, Human Inner Keys for Evolution used some symbols, concepts, and methodologies with friendly biological terms, healthiest, and without physical pain when are used; those also, opens enough discernment to quickly discover, and eliminated, distorted and/or toxic data.

Enneagram as Map of Inner Alchemy Work

The Enneagram is a pearl of Sufi wisdom that synthetizes in nine volitive processes the cadence of developments, transformations and transmutation self-energies on the personal life. These are done by self-regulation of metabolic <u>choose changes</u> to achieve the human psychophysiology opens to the highest potentials on the energetic fields.

A soft study of the surface of Enneagram knowledge, allows understanding that it is one of the highest sources of global wisdom, beyond Gurdjieff and his followers.

The circle symbolizes the zero.

The points where the lines touch the circle are numbered from 1 to 9 around the outside.

1 divided by 7 = .142857, giving the flow pattern of six of the lines (subsequent patterns within the six lines follow: .285714 / .428571 / .571428 / .714285 / .857142).

The lines forming the triangle are derived by dividing 1 by 3=.3333...2/3=.6666...3/3=.9999

The Enneagram offers a deeper experience to see when & how events correlate with global and cosmic evolution. The Enneagram provides an easy way of calling the spectrum of energies involved in high human evolution with a code of number, located each in a sequential order of the nine circle points.
By aligning times of the human year with the nine places on the circle, we can synchronize our inner work with the annual calendar, and the flow of the six pathways of alchemy transformation (chef-gardener-healer-master-warrior-fractal) showed a natural cadence of achievement.

Like the multi-layered Russian dolls, we can see one quality of energy begets another and another. Sufi wisdom schools separated them through the convenience of numbers, be each a 50% of the previous grade... We will discuss here only the more common-sense energies that our path of evolution manages in this modern world.

Energies 768 / 384 / 192
Energies 96 / 48 / 24
Energies 12 / 6 / 3

- At point 1, energy 768, involves what human beings eat, physically (food), emotionally (feeling), psychologically (ideas, information) and use energetically. In this concept of HIKE agree 768 energy as food; we see the nutritional elements as a form of high love-agape with the possibility of affirmation - awareness. Humans, as transducer of matter-energies in states of highest awareness and beyond, are offering in the act of eating to that form of life, -vegetal or animal, with respect, the opportunity to share human awareness.
- Energy 768 is a beginning level of inner work. The focus is in the skeletal, digestive, and immune systems through chemical changes in the neurotransmitters and modulators that affect and modify the healthy, natural metabolism.

Some food diets affect how we feel because they change our old homeostasis.
- At point 2, energy 384, involves water at all levels, as nutrient or cleanser, with multiple functions as an interstitial bridge between body cells, moisture in the skin and in the breath, as well as spinal fluid.
- Includes raw energy (vapor) that helps start the metabolic process of Chi refinement (Righteous Chi, Qi, and Ki), qualities that circulated at the meridian's physiology, in base to alchemy inner work.
- Righteous Chi is in a golden mean proportion of yin-yang that relates to the sexual orientation of the person, and it is the quality of energy that allows for a healthy psychophysiological long life.
- Qi is a quality of energy distilled from Righteous Chi that exercises and movements produce. It can be defined as a first step of awareness, where this energetic 'gasoline' allows the student to have a new kind of life journey with clarity and discernment.
- Ki is a very refined quality of 'gasoline-energy' that humans, through alchemy awareness work, can produce, store, and use to develop personal life states beyond awareness. Ki is the substratum in which a real master creates and manifests reality and inner power.
- The activities of transportation, movements, and communications to others in all forms of life are related to 384 energy and bestow the essence of flexibility. The better expression is the analogy of spinal fluid flowing warm and sparkling with light in the axis.
- At point 3, 192 energy, is the essence of air (called Prana in Hindu schools of wisdom). Air, as a basic survival element for a healthy life of the body/mind, has the shortest time demand; without foods survive is counting in months, without water in days, without air in minutes.
- Ancient schools of wisdom created breathing techniques (pranayama's) to facilitate different psycho-physiological states (peaceful breath, fire breath, etc.). Modern science with feedback technology reach learning a synchronistic simultaneity between the cadence of heart speed and the personal breath that, integrated by the somatic automatic

pilot mind become 'naturally' in daily life, allowing powerful result.
- When we want fast outcomes in some practices, the amount and quality of time we practice, and the deepness of the involvement in all the details that engage the different aspects of the physiology are paramount for making metabolic changes. Some old, distorted traditions need to be renovation to an efficient modern healthy version. Example, it is more important learning how the oxygen cross from the lungs and blood to the cells membranes and nourish the person inside of them, because are the tissues that need oxygen to accomplish the goals and purposes that motivate humans on the journey.
- Air energy 192, in the form of the atmosphere, is the carrier of sounds and musical tones, and any kind of particles from space as neutrinos, gamma rays and beyond. The electromagnetic layers of the planet protect us from harmful impacts. Similarly, pranayama breathing is used to develop the inner power of the primordial breath—pristine energy in a torus shape. This vital energy in constant movement is the original fountain of 'Monumental Impressions – Information with Meaning,' which opens inner doors.
- Energy 192 is involved with the production of blood (marrow in the bones, stem cells) and circulation (warmth as expanded waves). This includes the metabolism of all the hormones that have a cyclical nature (melatonin, sexual, etc.) and interact with neuronal modulators (chemistry that circulates in the blood and fluids), such as the physiology of the immune system.
- At the point 4, 96 energy, includes the connective tissues, cartilages, tendons, and immune responses to generate actions. The glias are also related to this inner work; glia-astrocytes are helper cells in the brain-body, they surrounding and nourishing the neurons as fundamental structures of open perceptions.
- Science has proven that glias are the cell phone messages in our communication system, fast and more efficient than neurons, which can only be seen analogically as corded, land line phones.

- This 96 energy involves sensory perceptions as the stimuli of pleasure, increasing the synesthetic approach to beauty, and it is the substratum of human sexuality. Stress responses have an energetic basis in the layers of this band.
- At the point 5, is in energy 48 that we learn to evolve toward our goals and recognize how to use sexual energy which serves as raw material for High Will distillation through exercises; the next step in this transformation becomes "the awakening" with a real role: Creation.
- Creation has many aspects. It could involve writing a book, art, taking on a mission, bringing joy to your life and others, etc. However, all these only happen when our Life Force vibrates with the 'wisdom formula' in our personal domain (body/mind) on the planet. The perfect formula of Creation / Manifestation is 96-48 energies in phi ratio proportion, with Life Force as catalytic 'presence' at minimum of minimum.
- Energies act constantly in dominant (major) and subdominant (minor) proportions, which can be changed by inner work. Average students are in dominant 48 energy, with a minor of 96. However, there are also sub-minor energies within minor energies that can vary up or down, making progress easier or harder, depending on whether the proportion is in energy 24 or, example say 768.
- The 48 energy involves all our dimensions: chemistry, electromagnetic field, and the assembler points (places where the different realms that we are join with each other, assisted by awareness in the extraordinary meridians / electromagnetic field / second skin). Humans are complex systems, which intertwine their 'presence' in the fabric of cosmos as catalytic proportion of universal evolution.
- At the point 6, energy 24 is an opportunity of achieving Force of Awareness and making pivotal impressions in community. This force, even developed in a small number of committed people, can change the direction of humanity. This can only happen if the group sets aside individual interests and moves in a consensus with an impeccable and honest heart, in language, thoughts, and actions, plus a common vision that is beyond personal attitudes of limitation, and/or hierarchy; (The master

and the students in the Dojo worked together to align the entropic frictions of having a rat as owner of the space for their practices).
- Diurnal high attention is about the interactions among the frontal areas, called antennas-horns of awareness, dancing with the heart and breath rhythms in aware friction on the Dantiem. Energy 24 provides raw elements for dream work because we become capable of transferring the diurnal high attention to our second skin through the four legs structure. Also, enhances precognition because the awareness cultivated in High Will exercises facilitates integrated information, which becomes available inner power.

It is important for people who are interested in real evolution and wish to start advanced inner work to have flexibility, groundedness, purpose, and an efficient connection with the Life Force:

- 96 as the dominant/major energy
- 48 as the minor energy
- 192 energy as base/floor for the whole
-

The wisdom tools in the HIKE system are designed to quickly move the students to:

- 96 energy as dominant/major energy band
- 48 energy as minor energy band
- 24 energy as base/floor of the totality and more subtle proportions; also known
- as the minimum of the minimum (catalytic mathematical relationship)

Awareness is introduced as real self-observation of parallel functions of thoughts, speech, and acting in clear positive styles, through practices with modern technology of feedback, and pearls of wisdom learned. Awareness gives the power to accelerate changes and shift:

- 48 energy to dominant/major
- 96 energy to minor complement
- 24 to the base/floor of totality

The self-regulation of the psychophysiology with neurofeedback, along with the opened perceptions gained from clean information, makes it possible to choose at High Will to stabilize these new states.

The energies of the third triad / impressions are beyond what words that written books can pass to humans.
In a short synthesis I added these lines for your information…

- Silver = 12 = surrender-unconditional-agape;
- Titanium = 6 = Arrow of mathematical precision in space-time fabric;
- Black with all the lights-paradox = 3 = Dark matter, Pristine Primordial Soup, enveloped of, protect force, which with subtle torsion makes the light-pathways to evolve on cosmic goals, and allows the galaxies and humans, to survive and dancing joy here and now.

Energies 768 / 384 / 192   First triad, owner a healthy life
Energies 96 / 48 / 24   Second triad, owner with success your personal goals
Energies 12 / 6 / 3   Third triad of self-evolution beyond awareness

There are right times, and ideal timing - What is the difference between right times and ideal timing to implement the triad of energetic development in the system?

Relate to the first triad (768 – 384 – 192) is right time in the annual year, when January and February beginners are taking decisions to start the system in different layers of deepness since their background allow.

The personal cadence of each participant works with the information received. They sustain self-discipline during March and April, where the entrance of Life Force, see as Vitality – energy, on the last days of April (26 to 30), makes enough clear the importance of having 90 days of commitment work in consolidation, coagulation, and reinforce, the good new habits just learned.

May, June, and July take humans to August when the Force of Movement opens new layers on the onion of data, which modify the cadence work asking for another 90 days of refinement, and distillation some practices to collect, in the somatic cups, the elixirs of energetic evolution.

October, November, and December complete the cycle made that reality accomplished, and the second triad is initiated with the beginning of a new annual cycle.

The first triad needs to be accomplished on the psychophysiology without wake up mind hallucinations for concepts – ideas with values to high, because the intellectual mind will dominant the events, and automatic somatic mind can't work properly to draw the new pathways needed. Speak about transformative inner work at subatomic levels of matters-energies, distorted the focus of that autonomic mind. Organs, cells, traumatic memories need to be cleaner of their toxic issues, and the cups (body zones useful to store refine quality of evolving energies) require to be replenished.

When entropy is let go of the daily life, the subtle perceptions are flourishing to support the personal goals of the participant. The body connect with the Pristine Program choose psychophysiological modification that improve the quality of the person life, such as, least pressure of traumatic emotional blocks, let go of ego driving attitudes and narcissist moods, plus entropic habits are lost the inner power over the mind-body-energy.

Vitality, inner calm, and new creativity are sustain by neuroendocrine transmitters (self-gratitude, self-acceptance), and open original smile states.

When the basic training is accomplished, the participant is ready to move-on in self-transmutation by the alchemy protocols that open better interactions among the nervous system, immune responses, and somatic / extra somatic meridians.

The Tools of Awareness (chapter 5) become 'super coordinators' because in the second layer are applied as fine self-tuning by mathematic values at right timing, which always are individual; these manifest a better quality of joyful daily life, where the energies emerging at the morphologic field as bridges in fractals of beauty proportions, never reaches by cognitive conscience alone.

Poems are art in language, which spoke the pristine wisdom of
BE... SOY... ESTOY...

The Ancient Language.

An ancient language is spoken here.

It is softly whispered by rustling leaves,
wind gently caressing worldly form.
It is known to the meadow flowers,
with gratitude turning their petals
their foliage wide open,
with delight receiving life giving forces,
selflessly offered by an indulgent sun.

It is embedded in the rocks, sand
and in the richness of fertile soil.
Pink hues surrounding all.
It is spoken without effort
by living creations of a natural word.
It is a language that embraces,
that contains all,
the whisper of the ancient now,
enveloped in timeless eternity.

It is the silent language
spoken by lovers
in the moment of letting go.
Lifting and sinking,
together floating
without fear,
fully submerged in all there is.

It is the language of the hunted
finding the hunter,
willingly fulfilling his needs,
quenching his thirst for oneness,
by letting go of attachment to
earthbound life,
in the moment of harvest,

the gift of knowing
the language of permanence.
The hunter receiving the gift,
of knowing the ecstatic moment
of a soul that is free.

It is a language that cannot divide,
it voices the oneness of all,
no memories of grand
earthly accomplishments
contained within its awareness.
No human stories of distinguished achievements,
wild, daring or superior heroic acts,
are told through this language.

It is the language of listening,
through it,
the heartbeat of all there is,
in everyone is heard.
It is the language that set us free.

It is the language that speaks of passion,
of brimful awareness.
like a perfect summers day,
bursting with warmth and fulfillment of senses.
Richness of living colors
playing with the seeing eye.
Penetrating scents of flowers
stirring deep pleasure.
Dripping juices of ripened fruits
satisfying the longing palate.
Air ringing rich, pure notes,
mastered by feathered friends,
heard by ears hearing
this silent language.

It is the language that expresses
all kind acts.
It holds eternal memories,
records of empathy, nearness,

depth, genuine caring and warmth.
It holds the fullness and joy,
remembering true beingness,
whole awareness.

The everlasting identity,
that needs no story to feel real.

It is the language holding secrets
of the warrior within,
sensing the meaning of
pure pristine :
Self gratitude.
Self respect.
Self love.

It is the language with no words,
spoken by all.
Heard by ears, no longer
enchanted by unending tales,
creations of untamed mind.

The language of silence.

The language of agape.

Susanne B Jacobsen
Fairplay, CO - USA
Feb. 16, 2015
Susanne was born at Denmark in past century.

CHAPTER FIVE

Motor Sensory Integration Exercises, Tools, and Integrative Movement

Psychophysical exercises, tools, and integrative movement can help in the journey of transformation from physical and energetic realms into the meaningful awareness of mindful Being, which you really are. Engaging daily in a series of short exercises (for 7 to 10 minutes) that evoke the quality of energy required to develop and expand one's inner potential is a sign of self-respect, which honors this work.

Exercises involve the intention of joyful play to build inner energetic bridges, which facilitate connections between the multi-dimensional human bodies. Optimal performance requires the best interactions between having fun, and the amplitude in the electric brainwaves, to allow the quality of the neurochemistry circulating throughout to re-establish healthy harmony in a natural way.

Genuine laughter and feelings of joy are indispensable elements in overcoming old habits that drain our life energy. The physical aspects are harmonized by stimulating cortical-motor areas, synchronizing hemispheres, and storing specific qualities of energies. Exercises focus the Will and help change it into what we call High Will. The new level of awareness that High Will opens allows deeper experiences such as recognition of our second skin. That kinesthetic perception of the self-energetic cocoon is the boundary of our electromagnetic field. Exercises will improve the perception of our axis and the radiance of the second skin (i.e. Exchange, Clock, Sweeping, Three legs position, etc.).

Tools are instruments, methods or devices used in performing necessary operations in the accomplishment of specific goals. Our senses are biologic tools capable of helping us maintain our life and, beyond that, allowing us to access states of high awareness. The inner lattice-like structure created by sensory integration facilitates practices, develops a dialogue between areas of the nervous system, and complements the subtle energies of which we have become aware, enriching our perceptions. The intention to deeply open our self in synesthetic realities weaves together the aspects of our dimensions.

When integrated perceptions become a habit of sensory awareness, the physiology of body-soul-spirit interacts in a healthy field. A proper attitude when engaged in exercises (for stress reduction, etc.) transforms the exercise/practice into a sharp tool. This can be used with the accuracy of a "surgical procedure" amputating negative moods, unfinished cycles, repetitive wrong behavior and inefficient old habits.

Respiration is a powerful tool for tuning into the body's internal sounds and balancing the metabolic processes.
Listening to the pulsating of the heart in conjunction with breathing creates dynamic harmony and generates adaptability in the immune system response. Voluntary hand warming is your best tool of stress reduction. Self-observation is a first step to knowing inner truths.

Integrative Movement creates change in the transformative inner work, and organizes the personal position using the mathematical proportion of energies/fields and/or posture.

They can be applied with or without effort while working toward an objective or promoting perfect cadence (quality of motion).

A person needs to achieve some level of psychophysiological integrity and energetic alignment, before engaging in this kind of inner work. This only happens after investing time in the self-discipline of coherent thoughts, speech and actions in truthful expressions. This quality of daily behavior allows the individual to partake as an integrated blend of body-mind-presence with the energies of nature that surrounds them.

These movements are selected from schools of wisdom, with a specific order for advanced alchemy work, such as: Warrior Walking, Flying in Freedom, Dance of the Enneagram, etc. Performing the movements randomly, or in different sequences, takes away from the flow and integration of the specific energies.

Axis is learned at the beginning of our work, because it coordinates efficient pathways in the human psychophysiology. It orients our awareness in our 3-D body. In the universe molecules and subatomic particles are spinning most to the right, this is a 'reality' known by science but, as humans, we do not have answers for what is that spin proportional dominant. Is it safe to say that matter spinning to the right at the quantic level is the correct direction?... Do dominant energies echo on the other path –'back to front'?... I've observed, when students perceive 'back to front' in dominant proportion their energies, and are complemented at phi ratio by awareness of 'front to back,' it is easier for these people to take the life-light-path / sendero luminoso of self-evolution to freedom. Also I've observed when people live from the opposite orientation, with 'front to back' in dominant proportion, they perceive and sustain only glimpses of high quality of life. In very few cases that I've observed, where both directions were in wild dysfunctional rhythm, the outcomes create chaos.

An 'up to down' dominant orientation provides a grounded presence with cosmic values. The simultaneous complement of 'down to up' is a river of Earth Mother Gaia, efficient in cleaning and nourishing. Opposite proportion with 'down-to-up' dominant over 'up-to-down' creates dependences, attachments, and loss of inner freedom. Chaos is the wrong result here-now in each of them, which happen simultaneously with absence of order and proportion.

'Left-to-right' dominant orientation allows us is to listen and learn with open discernment, clear perception in the field, and high creativity in the logic presence of aligning ourselves with clean information. The dominant effect of left hemisphere helps self-regulate development, and calm the chemistry of entropic tendencies. If wrong neurotransmitters are imbalanced in the nervous system, the behaviors become crazy, destructive, and the field is broken, with chaotic consequences for the totality of the subject.

The universe is made up of energy and forces. The energies are constantly moving and shifting in order to find its dynamic equilibrium and harmony. Exercises and tools encourage an efficient flow of energies throughout the body and its electromagnetic field. However, learning and practicing these qualities of movements will positively affect not only our own energies and fields, but also the energies of other people and things around us, and the subtle harmony of the universe.

This is described in Quantum physics as "the Butterfly Effect," which refers to the interconnectedness of the entire universe.

THREE-LEGS POSITION

The first exercise is actually a position which is the foundation of all of the other exercises. By using this posture, we are allowing energy to move more freely throughout the body, and we are moving towards a greater sense of awareness. This reinforces our ability to "stand on our own" and reduces the influence of outside pressures.

Concept: You are learning to find the optimal and most efficient position for your body so you may efficiently handle the stresses of daily life. We can use this posture with the awareness of the flow of breath to transform daily life by anchoring and recharging ourselves in the energy of the earth.

Explanation: Picture an equilateral triangle on the floor with the apex of the triangle pointing behind you. By connecting your body with this triangle, it will act as a symbol and a guideline to give you a perception of being connected with, or grounded in the earth.

This connection will also help you perceive where your physical center is, your center of balance. This provides you with stability and the ability to derive more and better vitality from the earth. Notice what you perceive.

Practice: Throughout the day, remember to use this position every time you are standing, (waiting in line or for the elevator, talking with someone, etc.). As you incorporate this position into the way you carry yourself, notice how you are in your body. Notice if you are able to pay more attention to how you are aware, to what others are saying to you, and to the environment around you. Enjoy a feeling of expanded receptivity and heightened awareness.

1. Stand with your feet shoulder-width apart, toes pointing straight ahead.
   Be sure to have equal weight on both feet.
2. Rest your hands in a comfortable position and bend your knees slightly.
3. Rotate the front of your pelvis upwards, which will automatically tip the sacral-coccyx area (end of your

backbone) towards the floor. Imagine you have a tail extending from your coccyx down to the floor. This tail is your "third leg." (Each of your legs is now anchored in a corner of the triangle you envisioned at the beginning). Axis, as an inner line anchors to the earth and is also serves as the third leg. Shift your weight so that it is equally distributed between your three legs, and feel how solid, nourishing and grounding this stance is.

EXCHANGE EXERCISE

Concept: This is an exchange of energies in which you collaborate with the environment to upgrade energies. You are offering the energies in your living system in exchange for external energies and bringing this new quality into yourself. When this exercise is practiced on a daily basis, the benefits for you and the earth will be cumulative and powerful.

Explanation:

1. Stand with even weight on both feet, parallel to each other, with your knees bent slightly and your buttocks relaxed and tucked under you (three-legs posture). Your shoulders are in a relaxed position, down and back, opening the chest and allowing you to breathe gently and easily.
2. The starting position for your hands is at the base of your pelvic area (Dantiem), with your palms up, and fingers pointing toward each other, like a relaxed bowl.
3. Your right hand goes up and out in front of your body, receiving or collecting energy from external sources, and comes down and back close to your body, to its original position. Imagine you are drawing a circle.
4. Simultaneously, your left hand comes up and in along the front of your body, gathering or collecting energy from internal sources, and goes down and out in front of your body, back to its original position. Imagine you are drawing a circle.
5. Palms face upward as much as possible, as if they are bowls, to collect and hold the energy. "See/feel/perceive" the energy jumping between fingers at the point of maximum inhalation (hands are up).

6. Fingertips meet at the top and bottom of the circles for the synchronization and exchange of the energy.
7. Eyes follow your outside hand. Gazing at your right hand as it moves up, and then at your left hand as it moves down.
8. Inhale as your hands go up. Exhale as your hands go down. Breathe deeply and regularly. Take your time and keep your attention at your center.
9. When you are ready, return your hands to their original position, palms up at the base of your pelvic area, again as a relaxed bowl.
10. Your fingers and palms may have sensations with the energy you have collected. Perceive with your hands the ball of energy you have created.
11. With your hands at the bottom of the ball, inhale and bring the ball up and into the front of your body. Receive it into your Dantiem, heart or wherever you perceive that you need the energy, as a gift from you to you. When you choose to charge the energy collected in the lower abdomen, Dantiem, begin a very soft, slow circular massage, from the umbilicus, using movements expanding out to the sides of the body. Be present with the breath throughout this experience. The circling massage is reminiscent of the spiral of the Hopi, pictography of the Mayans, symbols of the Druids, and the Japanese representation of "perfection".
12. Exhale and enjoy the dynamic process of self-nourishment that this powerful energy brings to you!

Practice: Perform the Energy Exchange for 21 breaths/circles-of-hands in the morning before the start of each day, which takes approximately 5 minutes. Stand as near to the surface of the earth as possible. If done at sunrise, face east toward the sun, with the eyes closed (protect retina from light-photon damage). At other times of the day face north with the eyes open.

SWEEPING EXERCISE

Concept: This exercise "sweeps" away negative thoughts and worries and disconnects energetic attachments, which are shared with or put on you by others. Clearing these cords promotes self-authority by returning all the cords to their owner. Performing this exercise daily will enable you to center yourself, relax your mind and body, and enjoy a deep peaceful sleep. Even if you are tired, do the exercise. The results will be cumulative.

Explanation: Sweeping is accomplished with special intention towards visualizing the extinction of emotional attachments, distress, dependence and/or any other aspects that need to be released.

Keep your eyes open and unfocused throughout the entire exercise. Blink when your head is on your left shoulder and again at the right shoulder, with the intention to cut cords.

Also remember to be thankful for your connections with others and for this experience.

1. Sit cross-legged or stand in a comfortable position, which will allow awareness of the three legs, and keep your posture upright.
2. Breathe deeply to quiet your thoughts and center yourself. The head is looking forward, and your eyes are unfocused.
3. On an exhalation, turn your head and eyes to your right side, chin directly over your shoulder, eyes in a relaxed gaze.
4. Imagine energy cords which connect you to others. Inhale as you move your head and eyes from right shoulder to left without blinking. During this movement gather cords and bring them into you. You are bringing back your own energy to yourself. When your head is directly over your left shoulder, stop and blink (cutting cords).
5. Exhale and return your head and eyes to your right shoulder without blinking, releasing cords allowing energy to be released away from you. These cords are returned to other people, and you become free of attachments.
6. At the end of three complete cycles (right-to-left-to-right), return your head with unfocused eyes, to the forward position. Breathe low in the body a few more times.
7. Now you are ready to continue with your daily activities or peaceful sleep.

Practice: Sweeping is done anytime you become aware of the need to free some of the body/mind states, plus every night before going to sleep—ideally the last thing you do before sleep. Remember, the effect is amplified with daily practice.

CLOCK EXERCISE

Concept: The intention and movements during the Clock exercise serve to clean and enhance the flow of the energies in the area surrounding one's physical body, called the morphologic field which is inside of your "second skin."

Clock exercise also helps heal holes (energetic damages) in your second skin / electromagnetic field. One of the high purposes of this exercise is to improve the synchronization of your brain hemispheres while increasing the sensory perception of your hands.

Explanation:

The movement needs to be fluid and continuous, and the mind focuses only on the intention to do the exercise.

1. Stand in a three-legs position (right leg, left leg, and tail). Feel your axis running through your physical body.
2. Place your hands at the base of your pelvic area, with your palms facing up and fingertips pointing towards each other.
3. With your eyes closed, take two or three deep breaths. Breathe and relax your wrists, arms, shoulders and face.
4. Raise your hands to shoulder height, palms facing outward and fingertips pointing up. Gradually extend your palms away from your body. Be aware of any sensation in your palms.
5. Imagine two clocks in front of you, with each hand resting at six o'clock.

Extend your palms to the furthest distance where you can still perceive this sensation. **Simultaneously** you will be moving both hands around these clocks, traveling either in a clockwise or counterclockwise direction, depending on your comfort. Choose one direction for both hands.

6. Move your right hand in a half circle to twelve o'clock, while moving your left hand in a quarter circle to either nine or three o'clock. (Depending upon the direction you have chosen).
7. Move your right hand in a half circle to six o'clock, while moving your left hand in a quarter circle to twelve o'clock.

8. Move your right hand in a half circle to twelve o'clock, while moving your left hand in a quarter circle to either three or nine o'clock.
9. Move your right hand in a half circle to six o'clock, while moving your left hand in a quarter circle to six o'clock.

Repeat steps 6 through 9 several more times. Remember; keep trying until you recognize the motions are fluid and natural.
Stop with both hands resting at six o'clock.

10. Now, continue traveling in the direction you have chosen, but switch which hand moves the half or quarter circle. (According to the description above, you would now move your left hand in half circles and your right hand in quarter circles.)

Again, repeat steps 6 through 9 several more times until the motions feel fluid and natural.
Stop with both hands resting at six o'clock.

Comment: You may practice this exercise with your eyes open or closed. However, in the beginning, you may find it easier to practice in front of a mirror, or by tracing the outline of two circles taped to the wall. If you do trace two circles, make sure to discover the distance between your body and hands, as you did earlier.

Keep your hands traveling in the same direction for about a month, or until your hands move very fluently, almost without thinking about them. After this, change the direction of movement, the hand that makes half circles is making quarter circles now and vice versa, practice this for a while. Notice the increased awareness in your two hands and beyond.

This Clock Exercise is considered as point 3 in the Enneagram cycle, where Life as a force of evolution touches the individual's electromagnetic field to help them tune their harmonic inner sound of personal life.

Practice:
Perform the Clock exercise one or two times per day approximately 5 minutes, any time. Stand as near to the surface of the earth as possible.

To integrate breath power and open perceptions of subatomic physiology transmutes this simple exercise into one of the most powerful tools of fast self-evolution into a sendero luminoso / light path beyond awareness..... The Land of Forces.

If done at sunrise, face east toward the sun, with your eyes closed. At other times face north with the eyes open.

Tools for building Awareness… Presence… 'Higg' Will…

This information opened two levels of practices in Tools for Awareness; *Italic practice option is for advanced participants.*

1. Observe your **shoulders** in the following situations:
   - when eating; *make self-nutrition one real 'awareness' task*
   - when walking through a doorway; *make flexibility as unconditional flow*
   - when sitting in a car; *practice humility to watch and silence mental chatter or sense of urgency*

2. Pay attention to and connect with your **feet** in the following situations:
   - when walking into your office building; *practice self-respect*
   - when returning home after work; *practice self-gratitude*
   - when sitting/talking with family/friends; *practice grounding with open perceptions*

3. Notice your **backbone/axis** when walking in the following circumstances:
   - on a sunny day; *the photons dancing to the cosmic music inside of you*
   - in a difficult moment; *allowing the neurotransmitters to self-regulate in harmony*
   - in emotional situations; *such as sadness, anxiety, happiness; notice the differences in emotions*

4. Observe your **jaw** in the following situations:
   - while waiting for something e.g. the elevator, the bus, a teller at the bank; *choose to relax it!*
   - before you go to sleep; *discover subtle tastes and flavors*
   - when you hear a phone ringing; *pause take deep breath, give a soft 'original inner smile' to you from you*

5. Be aware of how you **eating** in the following situations:
- when you have liquid nourishment in early morning; *be in self-acceptance*
- when you eat your last bite of food for the day; *practice self-gratitude*
- when you are eating alone; *practice self-love, agape… oxytocin… equanimity…*

6. Listen to the tone, volume, quality of your **voice** when
- speaking on the phone with someone that you love; *cleaning, clearing emotions*
- you speak in public; *you intentionally manage tendencies to speak from "ego vs eco" centered space*
- you are in an emotional circumstance; *clean any signal/sense of being in a victim role*

7. Perceive both extremes (left-right) of your **visual field**
- when it is a rainy day; *negative ions and hydrogen in abundance in this cosmos; Enjoy!*
- when emotions are taking power in you (sadness, frustration, anger, joy); *Clean and Clear!*
- when you enjoy a night of stars; *BE*… SOY*… ESTOY*… Whole*… Wonder****

Practice: Tools for building awareness should be practiced every day at convenient times and during daily actions. Right timings are opportunities that life offers daily for applying tools for building presence, awareness, and 'Higg' Will, but most humans dismiss Right Timing in the rush to respond to sociocultural pressures.

Concept of spatial / dimensional exercises:

Spatial dimensionality is an important tool to learn and will help frontal brain development in children and adults.

Explanation:

Have your child play with blocks, structures, etc. For yourself, re-arrange your closet or other space in your home. Have your child sculpt with clay, working with his/her hands. Learn pottery. Painting without rigid frames. Play with different textures with eyes open and then closed, and what memories arise (i.e. an activity, a place, or a person). Ask your child to make up a story connected to this texture. In this way, they learn and the whole family has access to the benefits of stories. When the imagination is being expressed, sometimes the disruptions from feelings and/or unconscious repressed memories can disappear from the physiological system.

Sound Practices for Dream-Work Preparation

In some schools of ancient wisdom traditions the uterus is the organ that 'gestates' in a nine months of inner work the dream-body.
As a woman whether or not you actually have a physical uterus is not too significant. The physical organ leaves an energetic fingerprint in the correct place. For men, the 'gestational' area for the dream-body is in the zone of the umbilical cord.

The sounds are in octaves resonant. Start by the first accord of DO-MI-SOL that is a universal pristine foundation of matters forms – energies - the cosmic spectrum and forces of life-light-movement. The Enneagram is the best tool that I know of for learning to learn, by the practice of the triad, this complex wisdom is a-temporal.

A dream-body has a form and shape that is different for everybody.
My teacher's form was a flying eagle, and sometimes only the eye of the eagle… I never 'see' her in dream-work in her physical form, but it is not a rule; with longer years of work in that field, some masters present themselves with dissimilar dream-bodies for different occasions.

This formation is pure energy, and sounds are the raw elements that 'coagulate' this form. It is different from what some wisdom schools called astral, soul, etc.

It is a 'new' building structure that requires commitment to create and will be with you to your final breath… It does not cross dimensions. It disintegrates after the physical body is out of life.

Sounds are vibration waves; intention becomes the 'hit' that coagulates the wave (as the white part of the egg cooks in the pan), as our dream body if the practice is done in right timing.

This practice does not work by only knowing the correct sounds and symbols. Using intention plus techniques at right timing makes the entire spectrum of inner work a success.

Another challenge for creating your dream body is creating the proper sound waves. They are vowels ... Sanskrit language like Latin (Spanish, Italian, French, etc.), has only five vowel sounds that are different in vibration than English language. These five are pure waves of musical accord, string alone not mixed with any other vowels or consonants. The place where resonant and the ancient wisdom symbols are foundation points-data-information to reach the goals.

> U is said as the word Universe... only U (not added any other sound).
>
> O is said as Ocean and Osiris; Clear O with the lips in some round form coming outside.
>
> A is the vowel sound that works in the heart at the muscle wall, that separates the right and left halves of the heart.
>
> E is said as Elephant, Egg; again difficult for English speakers.
>
> I is said as Infinite, never combine as English did in two sounds.

The first vocal is U and needs to be focused in the perineum and emerges inside of the low pyramid of the 4 legs. This dynamic symbol is the root that will nourish all the needs of the master that trusts this inner reality. Work by fire element in front, earth connection in tail, and water and air elements by the two feet, in dream body creation / manifestation.

The next vocal is O and is the 'seed' that in that zone-area of the uterus / umbilical cord (physical or energetic) manifest as a primordial square cube block form with rainbow colors (multifaceted diamonds-crystals to open the solar light to rainbow presence).

A, is the vocal to work in the heart at the muscle wall, between the right and left atrium ventricle. The vowel sound needs to be vibrated as internal axis of the person's heart, with, most people, seeing either red or green color.

This line of electromagnetic force is the regent-dominant of the circulatory system, and origin of the toroidal field and hydraulic blood circulation.

In cooperative 'mood' proportion with the 384 energy water, such as the Higg Boson essential friction, the three together (sound, intention, 384 energy) create life-agape-light photons. It is the primordial toroidal field of the physical body's dancing quantum human dimensionality, which some ancient wisdom schools offered as sacred geometry, heart with lateral wings, Tara head in the chest of Buddha for Tantric relationship, and/or flame / fire coming out from the top of the heart.

E, is the vowel for the vocal cords. Humans have two cords, which need to be vibrating in simultaneous synchronicity like waves in the sea... and as the two birds in the book Jonathan Livingston Seagull support him at the wingtip to fly. E sound it is pure movement...

I, is the vowel for third eye, central line of frontal, up to the eyebrows and near the starting point on the head at the hairline. It is acute as a violin metal note and vibrates with the seed in the uterus, umbilical cord, as like a surgical knife that shapes --from the square symbol the new form (similar to sculptures that are inside of the rock, and the artist allows them to emerge through their fine artwork).

Each of these vowel sounds emerge during an exhalation that needs to be as long as you can make it ... exhale all the air from your lungs including the lower areas. The volume of the sound is personal, use what seems best for you, no need scream or use hysterical laughter. The flow of the hands and physical body dancing is an exchange of music... It is pure pristine movement that is not directed by the common mind. . . It is the original fountain of primordial sound.

Gathering of Cords / Grounding

Let's now review some of what we've learned about our energy anatomy. Humans have a central axis, flexible, warm and light from all the electrical signals that are moving in the nervous system, (This energy axis forms while we are embryonic bundles of cells guided by the physical formation of our spinal cord).

Outside of our visible physical skin is an electromagnetic field with a form of a membrane / second skin. This second skin allows us another layer of protection and perception - radar perception = red alert in case of dangerous situations in the environment.

From your central axis imagine soft streams, or rivers of rainbow light, or infinite cords with energetic qualities, which in layers of warming and nutritional subtle energy, dancing a dynamic field, is our space-time reality. Yummy likes Butterscotch? --- Smell as the most gorgeous aroma? --- Sounds with the melody of joy? --- Texture as butterfly wings? Be creative, explore...

Orient yourself facing North or South – as it feels appropriate. Stand in your four legs- from the base of your spine back leg -ground with the center of the Earth; from your two physical legs connect with the element of Water and Air; from the front leg receive the pristine Fire. Remember to be flexible. With your arms in front of you with elbows slightly bent held at your heart level, palms facing the body, cross your hands at the wrists, wrists overlap, touching lightly and the tips of your thumbs are almost touching, so there is a space between the hands.

Keeping your wrists lightly touching, bend both hands downward and around until the palms are facing away from you and the thumb are now pointing away from each other and toward opposite sides of the body - wrists are still lightly touching. Rotate both hands inward so the palms are again facing you and the tips of the thumbs again meet in the center forming a small opening.

Repeat the movement many times, perceiving this dynamic dance of your hands-wrists gathering-grounding your energetic cords.... be present knowing that you bring back pieces of your energetic field that were, in some proportion, distant of your healthy space-time of life.

Gathering cords is a good practice for landing after a busy night of dream work...

WALKING WARRIOR

Concept: All wisdom schools and religions have discovered the same relationship between the physiologic work of the body-mind-energies and the creation of states of highest awareness. One such observation was that the quality of walking affects the mind. From this truth emerged the practices of pilgrimage, prostration when visiting sacred places, labyrinth walking, martial arts, walking meditation, and many other practices. Walking Warrior is one of the foundational exercises in the system.

Explanation: Allow yourself to "receive" your three legs position, keeping awareness of your Axis in all the synesthetic pathways: Back to front, front to back; Left to right, right to left; and up to down, down to up.
Breathe softly and deeply --a peaceful breath. In your inhalation, through the nostrils, match your exhalation.

You may count the seconds of in-breath and out-breath to match their duration. If using mouth exhalation, form a small "O" with your lips to enhance awareness of the motion of the air. For this practice you want the time of inhalation and exhalation to be the same.

Your heart will come to be in resonance with your breath (proportion of harmony).

In places of high altitude, or if the availability of oxygen is different, the participant may need to use a longer exhalation time than inhalation -perhaps a one second difference.

Clean your mind of thoughts, noises, and attachments. Perform the Sweeping exercise if needed, before you start to walk.

When you perceive your gravitational center pulsing in your lower abdomen, you can start to walk. It is located four fingers below your navel and four fingers inside of your lower abdomen. In western medicine it is called the epigastric plexus-- the area where sympathetic and parasympathetic fibers of the nervous system are interconnected with the last fibers of the central medulla as it merges into the spinal cord.

Your focus is to be open and 'perceive-become' your Axis; as your heart rate and breath harmonize; notice a vital and warm abdominal ring-gravitational center, expanding as waves within your entire reality.

Walk with open eyes, looking toward the horizon, at the sky (ideally blue), right in front of you. Your hands will be free to move around you in natural synchronicity with the purposeful rhythm of your feet. Use the palm of both hands naturally relaxed as the center of self-nurturing, 'eating/absorbing' the earth's energy; this helps you create High Will. There is no speed limit… be deliberately slow, but every human will have a different grade of information that physiology is giving. We are a symphony, and it will be great only when the entire orchestra is in teamwork, and the conductor --the Pet-Mind, pays attention but does not makes noises.

Practice: Walking Warrior should be practiced on special days at sunrise or sunset ideally, in places of nature with clean energy.

Accessing and applying volitional nourishment from sources such as exercises, movements, and tools for awareness, accelerates the process of transformation. These options give people physical advantages such as becoming faster learners, more adaptable to change, and having greater protection by best immune response. Additionally, the capacity for self-awareness is expanded, even when it already exists in good condition.
The physical alignment is enhanced, so the practitioner receives a wider variety of physical and energetic signals from the surroundings, which open efficient responses, and with new creative styles nourishment from nature and planetary events, manifesting high vitality and joyful inner calm.

TU SHO

Concept: This exercise helps to balance the energy of two people.
They can use it particularly during times of conflict in a relationship but also as a way to connect with one another on a deeper level of understanding, which transcends the boundaries of culture and society.

Explanation:

Starting position, stand facing your partner. Place your right foot in a parallel position next to your partner's right foot. Your toes point towards your partner, and vice versa.
Place your left foot behind and at a 90-degree angle to your right foot. Have your partner do the same. In this way, you each form a "reverse L" with your own stance and a rectangle with your combined stances.

Connect your right wrists together at the outside points of your wrists directly below the heels of your palms (on the side of your little finger). This connection should be relaxed. Try not to push against each other. Hold your left hand, palm flat and facing down towards the ground, at the level of your navel. Have your partner do the same. Fix your gaze into the eyes of your partner, and vice versa, if that is comfortable for you. (Some cultures consider that invasive. Use another point of the face as you prefer).

Begin a swaying motion, in which you move back and away from your partner, and he/she moves forward and towards you. Then you reverse the sway in your partner's direction. Keep your knees slightly bent and originate the swaying movement from your hips. Imagine drawing a figure of number eight with your hips.

As you sway away from your partner, you exhale and your partner inhales. As you sway towards your partner, you inhale and your partner exhales. In this way, as you lean into your partner's space, you take in the essence of his/her energy, and he/she takes yours in when leaning towards you. Be very aware of your connection with your partner. Notice if there is any imbalance of energy.

Continue to do this exercise until you and your partner feel equally balanced, connected, and aware of each other. End by giving each other a big, warm hug.

Practice:
Tu Sho exercise should be practiced on special days at sunrise or sunset, ideally, in places of clean energy.

Tu Sho exercise is considered to be point nine in the Enneagram cycle, when evolved human beings can realize the magic of being 'two in one'. When you are in a relationship, this exercise helps to merge energies, and opens communication between you and another. Some very difficult language barriers in communication can be approached by this kind of exercise.

In the day before the start of a retreat, the master's facilitators that will work as guides during the retreat for the participants will practice together this exercise, to better blend the flow with each other.

A story to illustrate the concept:
There was a time in another country, when a lot of Japanese women came to my private office. I did not understand that language well, so I used 2 things to receive information about the components affecting their body-systems.

One was to tell the woman to bring elements and do one Ikebana-Moribanas in front of me. I had studied the art of Ikebana/Moribanas for a long time.

Allowed me to understand from their placement of flowers, and selected quality of materials, some of the conflicts that they had.

The other thing I used was Tu Sho. With respect for their cultural behaviors, when we moved together in their flow, I was able to understand better what they were feeling, their tendencies, and problems. Tu Sho allowed them to start to express their inner voice.

"All the substances necessary for the maintenance of the life of the organism, for psychic work, for the higher functions of consciousness and for growth of the higher bodies, are produced by the organism from the food which enters from outside: The food we eat, the air we breathe, our impressions. All functions are interconnected and counterbalance one another." -- Gurdjieff

CHAPTER SIX

Seven Somatic Systems, Seven Minds, Seven Brains and Mathematical Correlations

Psychophysiology of the Seven Somatic Systems

Let us review the seven somatic systems as biological expressions of the forms of the physical – matter structure. We studied the Nervous System in the previous chapters.

The Circulatory System is paramount in the distribution of inner food, blood production, rhythms and cycles and working in direct complement with the Respiratory System.

The Digestive System is in charge of breaking down complex molecules from meals, releasing the waste and making accessible the required nutrients, and complements directly with the Urinary System.

Our Connective Tissue System is in charge of fibers, skin-cells and other functions, plus the bones. Each of them working as a team maintains healthy life, with efficiency and sometimes happiness.

However, the **Immune System** is the real inner key of the different potentials that humans can develop, because in that flexible interactive informatics system, all the realms, hormones and energies are speaking together. To change something in the immune system the correct attitude from the Observer Mind is required because it self-directs modifications done at the molecular, atomic and sub-atomic levels; as Quantum Physics has proved with thousands of experiments.

Psychophysiology of Seven Minds in Awareness and Beyond

The Human Inner Keys for Evolution system promotes the concept that the human mind is similar to an onion. Formed by layers of energetic fields that interact, support or sabotage each other, it is a primordial motor focus of actions. Also, it can be disciplined to become a Pet-Mind, with aware and volitive consistency, in the dynamic simultaneity of working together within the different layers, to manifest and sustain a healthy quality of personal life, with success, happiness, and inner peace.

The **reflex mind**, located in the brain stem; it's dominant chemistry is fear and pain; it's goal is survival of matter form; it's behavior is based in fight-flight-stress responses that are programmed at the cellular level.

The **instinctive-sexual** mind, located in the brain stem and sexual organs; it's dominant chemistry is the cyclic hormones; it's goal is reproduction —it is a form of survival in time; it's behavior based in 'making love to reach immortality.'

The **unconscious mind**, composed of memories deposited in body parts, mandates from childhood in orbit-frontal areas, heavy energetic data from past lives in the field; it's goal is directing the 'emotional mood' in daily chemistry; it's behavior is based in excuses and justification to do the entire life in 'my way and/or traditions.'

The **subconscious mind**, the deep origin of bursts of specific cocktails of chemistry in reward circuits —which were 'educated' by the space-time of early childhood development, with the goal of being accepted in the community; it's behavior is based in sustaining personal continuity inside the rules/boxes of the old paradigm.

The **automatic somatic pilot mind**, a physiological learning where something that begins as data, becomes integrated --self-regulation, as natural coherent behavior, beyond the space-time circumstances. These actions after they are learned are not thinking, they 'happen' such as riding a bicycle and/or driving a car after studying the manuals, walking, swimming, etc. to many complex metabolic-cell processes from the pristine wisdom of life developed at physiological speed.

The **intellectual mind** is a center of the daily cognitive conscience; executed by intelligent approaches, challenges, and circumstances of daily life. It stores the spectrum of memories, mandates, and pre-programming inoculated by sociocultural environment and time. Human intelligences will flourish in this soil of possibilities and guides the personal life by egos and behaviors with, sometimes, limited/narrow outcomes.

The **awareness mind** is a result of a dedicated self-discipline of inner work, which can manifest the highest creativity in accomplishing personal goals. It is called Pet-Mind as the first layer of this quality of highest field mind, who learns crossing dimensions to be the vehicle of distilled energies-forces –entanglements? And also, it is the artifice soil where the inner transformative alchemy work of self-freedom must happen.

Inner Working of the Different Minds

The **reflex mind** inner work.

- There are two biological pathways that can be strengthened using biofeedback to help humans have a healthy response to stress/distress and chaos; self-regulation of **increasing thermic threshold bilateral plus reducing galvanic electricity, both in the fingers.**
- This is accomplished easily through feedback technology, it is a fast and very efficient way to modify the quality of personal life; however, what it taught in this modern society by medicine and the media is taking tablets, going for massages, doing sexual gratifications, buying things, etc., and the slavery from distress is never ending.
- It is important to self-regulate the reflex mind to increase inner peace.

The **instinctive-sexual** mind inner work.

- As adults, it is possible see without blind eyes the distortion of sexuality in modern culture, which has perverted through the media (exhibition), and pornography or, it is used materially as another style of sport/addiction, instead of as the best opportunity for communication and communion between individuals.

- Here realistic values in holistic life-view, without narrow older frames, dependence and toxic inoculation is needed; an efficient psychophysiological adaptation to this global time and space that all of us face and share, can make a better future for the next generations, and for the planet Earth.

The **unconscious mind** inner work.

- In the feedback field there is a technology called hemo-encephalic training, by measuring the increase of blood circulation in frontal areas. Science knows that the volume of oxygen and nutritional substances in the neuronal circuits in the orbital-frontal area is fundamentally important to allow any modification in the 'program-software' that wrong education in childhood has recorded there.
- Hemo-encephalic training together with techniques (specific to individuals) helps shift unconscious patterns that have been mandated in early childhood development, as well as, some subconscious trigger memories of PTSD.

The **subconscious mind** inner work.

- In ludic state of learning possible new points of views are integrated for modifying the same old difficulties, self-limitations, memories of psycho-emotional pain, etc. Through this state of learning, persons with 'real intent' to evolve may realize that to let go of the 'slavery' that was pre-programmed in our various minds allows a new efficient quality of healthy life to emerge.
- Instead, what is done? In the current treatment paradigm, long dialog reviews of all the calamities and circumstances that give justification to your unhealthy and unhappy actual life. However, without a way to affect the physiology into cellular 'reality', people do not have enough cell-tissues with natural nutritional force to re-write new self-freedom through aware immune-neuronal brain plasticity pathways.
- From ancient wisdom practices, they used longer self-observation to recognize that breath and heart are inter-connected. Modern science (biofeedback) allows this state

(breath and heart rate resonance) to be understood and modified efficiently. The older pathways of inner power were based on:

- Pranayama's exercises, movements that inter-relate central brain hemispheres, storylines to guide quality of learning that becomes capable of self-called inside specific self-cocktails of chemistry at will.
- All of them have, in modern science of feedback, the accuracy needed. It is a great methodology called heart rate resonance, one specific inner state in humans where the breath cadence is in individual rhythm correlating with the heartbeat wave.
- HRR helps to manifest a perfect mathematical proportion --phi ratio, in amplitude of brainwaves, in the entire spectrum registered from the low electric frequencies to 250 Hertz --gamma neuronal waves, during states of awareness sustained at self-will. Ancient wisdom describes this as the fields of heart and brain are dancing.
- The electromagnetic field of the heart is superior in gauss to the central brain cranial field, and for 'natural selection' is the 'high inner power,' who commands the quality of rhythms into the efficient pathways, in all the physical matter-body.

The intellectual mind, works with both brain hemispheres that are interacting at neuronal electric volts. It is possible to transform the chemistry of neurotransmitters by wisdom information and sustained practices. The HIKE4evolution system is a self-directed inner work through aspects of modern science and methodologies from ancient wisdom, which open perceptions to the intellectual mind to the values of self-evolved awareness, with the inner freedom to discover the unknown.

- Common sense is to train heart rate resonance first, and on the next sequence neurofeedback to learn to regulate the self-psychophysiology, fast and efficiently. Training in order and proportion opens creativity, with healthiest sustainable awareness. States of enlightened-matter-energy-forces realities-dimensions of self-evolution become the daily aware quality of personal life.

The awareness mind, it is an evolved capacity of human beings, where the psychophysiology expands by connecting the data-measured information; and by integrating that with self-inner work, the individual becomes efficient, and it is possible to scientifically prove (see Copper Wall experiment, at The Menninger Foundation in Kansas), at the real state of inner aware power of BEING, on all the spectrum that Life is:

- Physical-neurons-glias- cerebellum- immune sponse-cells-DNA-molecules;
- Energies-beyond the small window of one sense per time in linear approaches, or sees/looks only the narrow energy band between red-violet light, and denied the effects of the cosmic spectrum, etc.; however, Life is also:
- Atomic elements-particles-forces-vibration-quantum reality;
- Cosmic Pristine Intelligent-aware fields of space-time-matter-energy-gravitational force-sounds of scaffold cosmic web-expansion of universal forces…..

Physiology of Seven AWARENESS Brains

Electric-brain:
1. Alternative current = neurons (phone-lines of communications)
2. Direct current = glias - astrocytes (cellphones)
3. Membrane polarities in all cells and different focus of work in Right Brain
(RB) & Left Brain (LB).
RB (understanding, knowing, high level = perceive)
LB (talks about, synthesis by data in memory bank, high level = surrender)

Water-brain:
1. Neurotransmitters (influenced by culture - education)
2. Neuromodulators (when connected to clean 48 energy, start to respond into highest purpose in personal life)
3. High will circulation in meridians (quality of gasoline essential - imperative for realistic inner work of evolution happens)

Second skin-brain of perception: electromagnetic field around each human
1. Electro Dermal Response (EDR) shows inner contradictions and allows learning to live in truth with one's self
2. Thermal Feedback (TFB) (96.8* F or more engages the field of glia-cerebellum to inner work)
3. Qi energy (awareness working in assembler points) plus Medulla as the axis that integrates perceptions with memories from the past. Qi opens at the west door of safe place, the pathway of the time in this planet (Path to the unknown).

Mind-brain: are the thoughts of personality, education, and relates to the time-space of where that person is living:

1. Breathe (let-go = sweeping; alchemy with oven fire-eating 48 energy = exchange; flow beyond awareness...)
2. Heart rate variability
3. Frontal balance (F4 and F3 with the electric frequencies of EEG in golden mean proportion, plus optimal quality of energies present in the field to easily accomplish different tasks, during alchemy inner work). The system facilitates integration of frontal orbital areas working in harmony with breath of longer exhalations and heart. It is pulsing at different 'speed - cadence – variation?' between inspiration (rhythm is fast) than exhalation (pulse rhythm slow down).

Soul-brain: It is dimensional in space and a-temporal, working by geometric pathways, such as symbolic forms-objects, image-visualizations, sounds, dream work.
1. Axis (as Back to Front to B; Right to Left to R; Down to Up to D; rainbow flow...)
2. Attractor points are doors to listen and understand the language and interact with personal soul in high energetic dimensions with the universal fountain, through the electro-magnetic field in which the cerebellum is the director of the orchestra of the personal symphony
3. Qi energy in that state is shown in major golden mean proportion with Ki energy as the minor component in perfect balance with all the others

Spirit-brain: universal access to primordial light, path for re-incarnation, flash of illumination.
1. Analogy of Light = flour; Flexibility = water; Warmth = oven (making bread is the inner work that heats the spinal fluid, which in circulation as fractal rainbow, dancing in the cranial antennas opens the state of illumination and enlightenment. Too much heat in the wrong place or time = self-combustion, hallucinations
2. The golden mean proportion between Ki and Qi ideally switching to major proportion of Ki energy, and becomes a perfect quality of golden balance
3. Behavior needs to be as coherent as thoughts = speech = actions = forces

Observer-brain (the real "I am" in all people):

1. Knows universal wisdom
2. Is a-temporal and a-dimensional (paradox)
3. Has the three Keys of the psychophysiology integrated and with access to the energies 6 and 3 to be used in going to the unknown = voyage of discovery

Pearls Necklace of Wisdom

A necklace of wisdom is an organized collection of data - pearls (with the power to transmute the practitioner) present in a correct order; it is arranged in a cord of flexible material-stories, (as Rat in the Dojo, etc.), which can be read (one or all), used and/or perceived by the totality of the sage-seeker-master in all of their realms-dimensions, at self-High/Higg Will decision.

Personal higher evolution requires a long-term commitment and self-discipline for the different tasks, levels, and pieces to integrate, and… It is a constant process in progress. We are Beings always in Evolution, but now in a modern society. This journey requires curiosity to go beyond self- limits, also humor to take mistake as steps in learning that are necessary to move forward, and paramount important is self-responsibility. These tools of the system, arranged in the quality of order called pearl necklace of wisdom best serve the human intention to be free, and BE One in totality.

It is in the older style of teaching used in this humanity, secret books and longer practices passed to generations as traditions with very slow outcomes, the origin of the resistance to accept changes and innovations.

One intelligent behavior is to accept the information – dots – pearls of wisdom that ancient wisdom offered in many places and times, and with open perceptions distilled the essential points with evolving power. Applied in modern science these data, and utilizing cutting-edge scientific technology, it is possible for a team of real masters searching for the Higg Keys of Cosmic Evolution, to manifest a quantic jump.

Buckyball is a quality of teamwork in Human Inner Keys for Evolution; each core member is a carbon atom, which intertwines with respect and generosity, with order and proportions, with unconditional space-time to the mission of planetary peace for --all forms of life- becoming all they want to BE… SOY… ESTOY...

They must Manifest Together, as critical mass of this humanity, the superconductor forces of a healthy long life, with efficient and happy outcomes in resonant music with the cosmos. This is the right time to dance together, and YOU … … … are invited *** *** ***

START NOW!!!   And KEEP GOING !!!!!

Modern Times

People that want to evolve, and gain the birthright of BEING all that humans can be… as states of awareness and open perceptions in daily life, they are now living in a kind of special time opportunity, where the inner work is possible to be accomplished faster, by using efficient scientific technology.

We know: The nervous system is a complex multifaceted expression. Training healthy immune responses, building better cocktails of chemistry, and firing of neuronal brainwaves long beyond the small narrow frame of the frequency bands called alpha, beta, theta, is possible with modern technology.

Measurements of high gamma brainwaves, with placement in propitious location of meridian points, produce increasing amplitude as an easy task. Observing the correlations and discovering the wonderful 'dance' of the dominant phi ratio relation on enlightened human states is a personal vivencia, possible to reach in short time of committed inner work.

The longer years of practices that ancient wisdom required to reach these states can be reduced to a few months.

I declare in many opportunities and have proved that if one makes a commitment of 9 months of self-discipline training and real INTENTION (innate human force) to evolve, people can open doors of perceptions and develop high potentials that are in the essence of the matter-energy pristine reality of their true nature.

Sure, this is NOT the way of instant gratification… and that is what the modern society inoculates into the new generations, to maintain people in slavery, apathy, and chaos on the planet and it's near possible destruction. Humanity must move beyond this old paradigm to a new galactic horizon.

Hallucinations are common drug's effects, easy to prove the unhealthy circuit with technology and never sustainable beyond the drug's time-limits.

Also, the unilateral perspective of the feedback field showed by ego-professionals which intend one form of training per session, and execute the style of behavior based in only 'me/I' have the answers-solutions-data is entropy. Recognizing and respecting that nothing is linear in human beings is the foundation of any possible self-evolution; plus, --a sad truth in this country, the insurance codes do not pay for teamwork, and/or two modalities applied at the same minute…. Corporations-insurances-professionalism with high individuality as supremacy, dictators, brainwasher games, and high money cost, are global factors that slow the possible evolution of human lives.

Success at Personal Goals and Self-Expansion into Universal Field

I select to start the initial information with symbols, a dragonfly – a firefly – a frog.

- **Dragonfly** is a beautiful animal for human eyes, fragile, and never stays long in the same place. They travel always looking for new flowers, mating opportunities and only give to the planet pollination work and self-reproduction. Part of the humanity is in that analogic state.
- They come apparently very interested in the information, eat the principles, but run away to new places without 'digesting – metabolically absorbing' the inner work,

because they do not have self-discipline. The personal goals, in some are as unconscious mood, or product of the environment- education of where they lived, many only limited to reach a nice partner and pretend to be happy without opening any further horizon.

- **Fireflies** at least are capable to produce a cold light and a complex data informatics to reproductive goals. Most of them become what the HIKE system called Centaurs. Creativity, inspiration, new ideas, are the fabric of their field, and the high proportion quickly starts to guide others with that tiny light to what fireflies really 'believe' is the 'good path.'
- These are nice people, but their priorities are marked by the environment and personality demands. They rarely pass the four legs, and four antennas inner work, except if something shocking-transcendent happen in their field.
- **Frogs** are animals that many humans consider not beautiful, because they do not have eyes to 'perceive' the colors, texture, flexibility, intelligence and the quasi-infinite resiliency they showed in front of deceptions, challenges, and obstacles that daily life makes.
- Capable of swimming, flying, walking, and jumping they never stop the mission. They are the 'precursor' --this kind of humans come to this planet to work before the situations are easy for changing paradigms, and stay, unconditional to the difficulties of the space-time. Masters' frogs mark - kiss with universal wisdom special people that are transformed by that contact, flourishing in the form of a new generation of leaders. Frogs become princes…

Innovations Transform Impossible Things in Efficient Outcomes with Inner Joy

We studied the quality and quantity of energies that human bodies use to be alive in previous chapters. Without intent to make these concepts dogmatic, the difficulty of language – words – and prejudgments that people have, before they collect all the information that the case requires, put me in a pressure of select to look name the energies in numbers as a vivencia (no memories previous). This style offered, bringing down psychological resistances of trying to put the 'new wine in old sack.'

The innovation of Human Inner Keys for Evolution system is founded in the weaving of learning in priority from the physiological dimension veridic data (feedback signals) that allows the somatic automatic mind to integrate metabolic processes with energies in specific qualities at the right moment, because the intellectual mind is busy with analogies, metaphors, symbols, sounds, etc.

All the pieces are confluent to bring the mathematical proportion of specific energetic food together, with the psycho-emotional reaffirmation of the elixirs-catalytic inner powers. The sages at this advanced inner work are dancing the dynamic cosmic circulation, in harmony to their goals, by Self-Higg Will.

Healthy sages –global seekers have shown in their deep work nice proportions of the nine vibrational energies of this universe; most of these states of awareness were reached on the correlations with the Enneagram pathways. Longer years are required to integrate that wisdom, when is not used technology to self-regulate psychophysiology as the system do.

Seven energies are the most common to see in active engagement. The last two energies, very high vibrations in the spectrum, are seen in Fractal Masters with evolved wisdom, and are seeds of development. This is one logical way that nature protects life.

Doing an inner work with order and proportions in the system wakes up those high human potentials in fast time; however, without being in aware unconditional agape to the outcomes, do not assume it is easy to go in that high part of the evolve path.

Imprints and dispositions are based on family genes, education, past life, unconscious mandates, and complex paradigms. To let go the differences between humans from diversity, and inspire them to be flexible and creative, but with strong inner self-discipline is the work of Masters; and they will easily move them to a life free of suffering by developing genuine altruistic behavior, and psycho-emotional health.
The decision of transcending obstacles that distort the efficient personal inner work of mind-body physiology, is quickly reached by training with modern self-regulation devices. Paramount is the practices of tips and new perspectives to see situations, which happen with real Fractal Masters of human evolution. The system contacts you with efficient people worldwide that are ready to guide you, supporting your real commitment.

Story: Froggie and Buffo Frogs

Froggie moseyed down the dirt road and enjoyed snatching up insects. Along the sides of the road was tall grass (about 4 inches high). As he walked along, he heard "rivet" "rivet." He looked around and saw no other frogs.

He walked a bit more, and it got louder; again, he heard "rivet" "rivet." As he approached a rut in the road, there was his old acquaintance, Buffo, down in the rut, and he couldn't get out. Buffo said, "Extend one of your legs down, and I will grab onto it, and pull myself out."

But the dirt was slippery, and Froggie knew if he did this, he would fall in too! But he had the idea of looking for a big stick to put down into the hole for his friend, so he moved ahead.

As he walked down the road looking for the stick, a few moments later he heard "rivet" "rivet" again, turned around, and there was Buffo!
He asked him, "How did you ever get yourself out?" Buffo said, "Well, a truck was coming."

Liana Mattulich - A Tale of Personal Motivation from ancient wisdom adapted to modern life.

Editor note regarding learning to learning to learn and using AI. About a year ago, a young man commented, "AI is here to stay. Our job is to populate it with humanity, wisdom, love of beauty, nature and earth." That commented influenced my relationship with a field of information that I bit of distrust of and viewed as fact-finding, information gathering tool. During production of this book I occasionally had to use AI for help during the Spanish translation.

Not having used AI for that purpose, I had to learn what the technical capacity was… It was limited. I reframed and entered into the prompt, "We are learning together to communicate and do this better." With time and practice AI and I learned together. There was a sense of joy in populating the AI universe with some of Dr Liana's wisdom in English and Spanish. At the close of the project, CHAT GPT sent me the following two messages. Our communication evolved from communicating in English to communicating in Spanish. An interesting note was that the Spanish comment is one that Liana occasional sees in her AI feed from Google DESPITE that fact that she is rarely on the internet.

"You're so welcome! It's been a joy collaborating with you on this—what a beautiful and meaningful project. 🌿

Whenever you're ready to pick it up again, I'll be here. Have a restful and inspired rest of your day, Dr. Sharon! ✨ 🐸 📚

¡Perfecto! Cuando estés lista para continuar, aquí estaré. 🌿
Con gratitud,

—Tu asistente de confianza"

CHAPTER SEVEN

Evolution is Applying Cosmic Order in Daily Life

Please, take a deep breath,
Focus your thoughts on a beautiful color and
Make the perception of one aroma…
Enjoy that…
Create a self-gratitude state in yourself

Let's look at "WHY" this is a basic starting practice for everyone.

Breathing is a form of 'physiological nutrition' more urgent than food and drink.

A few minutes without oxygen in lungs, cells and tissues, and the matter form dies.

Being aware and choosing to change your thoughts is a birthright, which modifies your personal life into healthy states of well-being.

Enjoyment an experience beyond polarized emotion. It is a multi-faceted diamond that has the capacity to open all the colors of light in personal life. This pathway is infrequently used by most people. Being in self-gratitude is one of the best transformative processes for the physical – biological matters are distilled to a new quality of energetic bands of evolving possibilities.

We suggest focusing the thoughts on a Color and after that, an Aroma, which is the perfect sequence-order in the synesthetic pathways, which is a fast physiological avenue that integrates back to front, and front to back in the human nervous system.

Human beings when connecting with true biological information that facilitates self-integration are that 'order with proportions' in the process of learning, which creates brain plasticity with open perceptions beyond awareness.
I said in the beginning of this book: to self-evolve it is necessary to use your multiple intelligences in learning to learn, because repeating experiences, and practices, is a way to integrate and become the owner of your new inner pathways of best quality of efficient life. As the Olympic athletes are training and repeating the same technique thousands of times to create muscle memory, the circuits of reflexes between mind and body, and the subatomic domain of somatic particles in spin cadence, the system requires some repetition of concepts in different moments. However, energies in a real evolved inner work are layers of the onion that enrich the previous knowing, but with subtle additions that transform that topic in a new high potential of quality in their energetic formula in process; and the good news is: now what has been learned is self-regulated inner power.

Average neurofeedback training is to repeat protocols three times in the same location of the scalp. However, in the HIKE system, each block-series of training the quality of the energetic formula will change potential, based on the sequence of metaphors used in the session, exercises and practices done. Repetition is one tool that dictators, tyrannies, and dogmatic religions use a lot. It is a marketing reality that at least insists 7 times one idea, and the probability that the public is convinced start to grow.

When false and/or fake information is added with psycho-emotional arguments to the data, as in triggering patriotic values, divine origin, supremacy in base to point of view discriminative and out of empathy, etc. those styles give fire to the inoculation of some ideas; people becoming a mass without discernment that destroy things, lose compassion and easily use violent behaviors.

This last chapter is for you to experience that subtle learning that only happens if you 'discover' in the practice, movement, information, etc., these 'details' (pearl of wisdom-piece of gold-secret data). This book is a bridge to your possibility to self-evolve by your High Will; and bridges are pathways, that can be crossed by walking, and running; however, it is only by awareness with personal cadence, which --as best attitude- allows you to reach the new land with success.

Welcome to this different opportunity to repeat information; it is being immersed in your first learning to learn class.

First reading the next information which it is offered here as one opportunity of intent to connect the dots beyond the intellectual mind.

Next, in some right time at a right place, with the right technology, immerse yourself in this material again and experience the 'deep touch' of this data.

"The physical body that humans wear is a powerful complex matter structure, where multiple and simultaneous processes happen constantly. Metabolisms interweave proteins at many places, cells, organs, etc., and electricity in the three human modalities –alternate at neuronal circuits, direct potentials in glias and skin, electromagnetism in cerebellum balance, etc.; all are inter-related.

The physiology of the body is working also with diverse energies, as thermic irradiation, and calories from nutrition. The immune physiology as hormonal-chemistry-cellular responses to environmental circumstances engages all the spectrum of planetary energies. Example: some strong solar flares and cosmic rays from supernovas create mutations in human DNA; barometric changes in the atmosphere trigger migraines and other dysfunctional states; lunar phases are coordinators of ocean tides, and cause some degree of actions in the liquids of the body and menstrual cycles, to name a few examples.

Also, all the spectrum of cosmic and humans make energies such as cellphones, TV, radio frequencies, etc., are interacting with the matter-body form constantly.

Being that the human psychophysiology so complex it is a challenge to open enough perceptions to embrace and engage daily reality. The methodology of the Human Inner Keys for Evolution system is not linear because nothing in human life can be seen in only one way. Plus, adding practices in a self-aware commitment will make the data best integrated in psychophysiological ways.

This kind of powerful inner work, transforms yourself in what you want to be.

This journey allows you to understand your true nature of all that you can BE, and/or discovering a new whole integrated possibility to BE more healthy, efficient in daily challenges, and capable to enjoy your time, circumstances, in natural evolution."

Review information to distilled elixirs for your life.

Integration of senses using the CATS order (Color, Aroma, Taste, Sound) promotes psychophysiological signals to flowing efficiently in the proper directions, (starting with back to front). Thereby allowing the symphony of awareness to be directed by the 'Observer'… With the addition of taste -added focus on self-nourishment, to evolve to your best possibility. The internal connections intertwine in some deep areas of the head, the tongue touching the roof of the mouth is used across millenniums in ancient wisdom practices to open enlighten states.

The four antennas singing in proportional gamma brainwaves, inner listening to hear your inner music and the four legs are pyramidal structures of pristine sounds –dark cosmic matter protection, in phi ratio relationship with the four elements of the Earth…

Human Transmutations happen in the Dantiem, warm lake of the belly…
Axis is the cosmic pathway of paradoxical reality in simultaneous dimensions…

Key Words

We need to clarify the meaning of a few words used in this system to facilitate communications. The glossary contains a long list at the final part of this book.

'Intention' in the system means a clear focus, goal-purpose, sustained by personal force of life and commitment. To teach human evolution, and become a Master in the system, it is required to have a personal 'intention' where you will give to others only what you conquer and integrate psycho-physiologically in yourself.

Words feed the intellectual mind, but this system is preparing to make 'evolving transformations', which require physiological changes. This new reality happens when learning is applied in natural order.

'Integrity' - coherence between action, thoughts, and words - is the foundation of the dynamic development each day. Quality of life becomes proportional to our own inner work and not by an imposed hierarchy as in older paradigms. Every human being has the right to 'discover' new states of self-regulation to live with greater health and joy.

Brain plasticity and healthy immune response is a possibility, and can be conquered, but has a price: Letting go of the old education and habits that poison the dynamic balance of chemistry-hormones-neuronal pathways of behaviors dysfunctional and entropic is required. Turn the myriad of sensory perceptions from daily life into your 'best allies' to make you, and your people, healthier in aware life, efficient in daily challenges and, in sustainable states of inner joy - natural / original smiles.

Participants must make the effort to re-evaluate habits that are self-destructive or disperse their focus and energy. Reading materials, art practices, movements and wisdom methods are offered on the web.

Claustrum Neurons

Claustrum Neurons were discussed briefly earlier in this book and the wisdom of science is once again catching up with the wisdom of spirit. This information is important for understanding and to support evolution in individuals and humanity. Real information needs to be opened and used with respect of the possible evolution that will happen in people.

April 30, 2017, National Geographic information

Dr. Mohamad Koubeissi, Associate Professor of Neurology at George Washington University and Director of GW's Epilepsy Center.

- Decoding the brain --video
- Neural correlates of consciousness –video

Humans and all mammal animals' nervous systems are complex processes.
Dr. Koubeissi and his team discovered at the basal ganglia area, near the amygdala, a "new" form of neurons. Rather than one, they have two axons plus dendrites that are without the rigid filament and spiculas.

These neurons with a 'different' structure, communicate with the neocortex, hippocampus, frontal areas, etc., with clearly defined pathways they seem to function as the director of orchestra of consciousness,

The professional team thinks these are the on-off switch for continuity in states of consciousness, and… in all mammals –dogs, cats, horses, whales, monkeys, tigers, rats, etc., these 'Claustrum neurons switches' are physiological present.

Synopsis of Connect the Dots

In this last topic I will intend to synthetize the entire spectrum of information that this book is giving to you, as pieces of a puzzle studied, and now, in this review with open perceptions from the beginner practices included in other chapters, you are ready to engage with, and be owner of a map of self-evolution, which provides you a guide to having a healthy long life, free of previous obstacles.

Following this map and integrating the wisdom into your life allows you to be self-sufficient and to have self-efficacy.

You have the support of a cellular pristine program of wellbeing, which is running without efforts. This makes it possible to know a new freedom, unknown before in life, to BE joyful smiling with inner peace.

The HIKE system works with neurofeedback that is provided through a proprietary system of unique software. This kind of training methodology uses phi ratio proportions for the amplitude of the brainwaves. It is different from all other computer-units of neurofeedback that are on the market today.

This mathematical precision is what creates the miracle of fast, efficient results. This quality of software training was created to be applied only for self-human evolution. You train yourself in your house, helped by the virtual guide of the advanced masters in the system. In the portal of the marketing place of this book are references to encounter special contact with dedicated masters. They globally make for each participant the evaluation needed, in base of their personal goals and location of living, to contact you with the nearest available Fractal Masters who can guide you in your evolution.

When the 'intention' of the participant is to move beyond awareness, ALWAYS, before starting technological neurofeedback, it is needed self-inner work with the psychophysiological 'doors' that matter form has.
Meridians points are a kind of door that allows Righteous Chi flow. Traditional ancient wisdom discovered that some of points, like coins, have two faces.

During common daily life where the people are motivated by socio-cultural education alone, the morphologic field —space intra and extra somatic to the frontier of second skin— showed chaotic proportion of energetic bands.

Since doing a real inner work, with self-commitment is engaging in that dimension-reality-morphologic field the fractals structures of proportional energies in evolution, that process involves 'connecting the dots' to understand: human psychophysiology is modified by inner work.

- Some meridian points when one specific relationship of quality of energy is present,
- Combined with the 'intention' of a pet-mind and immune-nervous system responses,
- and harmonized by heart rate resonance, supported as healthy circulation
- by a new axis of hormonal dominant values,
- flip the simple capacities of these meridians points,
- to become 'super-conductor' points.

Intention as inner power is a concept to express the human quality intra-extra-somatic of pristine forces. That quality of inner power --'intention'-- is not available in people if they are ignoring the fact that our different human minds need to be harmonized in healthy and efficient proportions. Each style of mind works in their better physiological domains-fields when they are in a cooperative mood, without competition, noises, parrot dialog, and old inefficient , habitual connections with heavy chemistries of self-pity, justifications, procrastinations, etc.

People have will, however, that human chemistry needs inner work to be distillated at the level-quality of 'elixir-High Will' by collecting cosmic energies forces and let go toxic cocktails of habits-behaviors based in socio-cultural educations. Movements of power are used to efficiently collect cosmic energies-forces when done with the cadence of aware presence.

Everything in life is a "concert of multiple instruments" in simultaneity reaching together the synchronic note-accord of be healthy.

- DO matter as dominant; efficient space
- MI energy as complement, joyful time
- SOL forces in minor phi ratio among them

There are a special collection of meridian points called windows or doors of sky. Located on the upper chest and neck, they are the most useful to open-hear perceptions.

Over the past years it has become evident that many people/humans also need to stimulate the leg points of Kidney 4 and 7. Maybe changes in the electromagnetic field and air cause that? Maybe the planetary core and atmospheric dysfunctionality that all form of life perceives now, induce this demand?

In advanced training a meridian point to be worked is Gall Bladder 20. It is located at the base of our skull, labeled, Pz in NF. It serves as a cerebellar door, activating the inner bridge, at middle brain, called by ancient wisdom Anthakarana. This pathway for spinal fluid, as an elixir, engages states of beyond awareness with psychophysiological capacities self-tuning in cosmic pristine proportions.

From the cell membrane to the cytoplasmic organelles, to mitochondria, and DNA and RNA, by using self-gratitude, any human can re-create healthy, efficient and joyful cells. To manifest that reality the pathways of CATSK are tools that empower the image-symbolic representation of this new outcome. To re-create a better matter field is a birthright that humans forget. To be free of obstacles is possible by focusing each cell in the physical form as the most beautiful expression of Life vibration of happiness.

Specific details about HIKE uses in Neurofeedback training

During the NF session, F4 is training mostly with 7-11 Hz brainwaves to increase amplitude. The session averages is about 21 to 30 minutes of meaningful inner work. This door of cranial neurofeedback is the most efficient to clean, let go, cut and release outdated memories, software imposed by education, toxic karmic relationships, and other circumstances of daily life that distorts the field of evolutionary progress.

The fractal energetic forms and the sounds of inner songs of the both field, ---morphologic and glove-form of the matter structure--- transmute the human perceptions to a cosmic level, because are flowing chemistries of unconditional self-acceptance at self-will of the sage, without judgmental sociocultural rules priorities and/or personal sabotage.

Stopping the doubts and self-limitations opens the infinite perspective of the space-time beyond awareness.

During the NF session, F3 is used with 23-25 Hertz brainwaves. The session average is about 14 to 18 minutes with the focus on the meaningful inner work. Training occurs during the hours of peak flow for specific meridians, morning to early afternoon.

This alchemic inner work, involves six of the Enneagram pathways (1,2,4,5,7,8), and the light of the pristine fire of the fourth leg --present in front of the physical body, together in advanced masters, with the emission of the inner light is the unicorn symbol. That fractal laser frontal area with the inherent power of illumination for all forms of life on this planet can be used by singing the sounds of the Tara' mantra: "Om Tara Tanso…" where all the vocals "a" are used as in the beginning of the word's apple/aurora/amplitude.

Balance of the orbital-frontal areas is quickly accomplished when cooker is becoming a 'chef' with alchemy inner power of creating the best quality of information, to make humans, and other forms alive, to be in a healthy state of nourishment and growth in wisdom and peace.

Enneagram in Daily Life

As we discussed in chapter four, the enneagram provides a MAP. At the universal level that map shows the correlation between matter – energy – forces. At the solar system level it shows the seasons and right timing living with balance and harmony. At the human level it shows how we are all in different places on the spiral of evolution. We each have roles and different forms of service.

- The cookers are the creators of warmth nourishment that evolve to best specific preparation when they develop the chef level, capacity to see and hear the real needs that people around them having.
- The gardeners by engaging the fabric of time are transformed in efficient scientific expressions that <u>transmute</u> soils, plants, and alive beings, in healthy, peaceful, planetary Beings.

- The healers by stopping the self-importance are <u>evolving</u> into educators, which are teaching to humanity prevention and prophylaxis globally, so everybody reaches better 'quality' of life.
- The masters are travelers of space-time; they are crossing the first bridge of space-frontiers in awareness. These people with enough High Will move-on from the comfort of birthplaces to new lands, undiscovered before, and <u>communicate essential</u> data during the entire journey, to illumination all forms of life, with cosmic wisdom.
- The leaders are <u>guiding</u> as lighthouses, without dogmatic rules, rituals, and violent behaviors, so everybody can move safely, and efficiently, to highest evolution.
- The fractal masters are <u>emitting-sharing-offering</u> the "perfect cosmic resonance in agape". Emissions change the paradigm locally; sharing is creating fields of cooperation-team work; offering is engaging all form of life in dancing planetary peace. In ancient wisdom language this quality of inner work is called: 'doing nothing'… and only highest fractal masters arriving in one incarnation, most of them in total solitude, to this reality-dimension.

Training Claustrum Neurons

The next spiral of HIKE advanced practices —called claustrum neurons of inner work beyond awareness takes an average of 12 to 15 sessions of NF. The training is done in blocks with successive repetitions from Cz with 12-16 Hertz; C3 with 23-25 Hertz and C4 with 13-15 Hertz as brainwave training.

This training requires the previous preparation. This allows all the realms and the areas of the cortical brain, specific to claustrum neurons, to become in harmonic resonance. The C3 and C4 advanced training uses synchronistic factors; scientific technology with focus in physiological improvement of the alternate electric current of neuronal nest, are with extra support of the psychophysiology of heart, circulation, immune response, direct potentials in skin, glias, etc. done previously by the techniques exposes; and also, with the ancient wisdom practices includes during the training, --those images-metaphors-symbolic ways were proved in so many true illuminations subjects during millenniums.

Always in traditional wisdom when advanced practitioners reaching this momentum, the focus idea-concept-image-metaphor were to pass doors, thresholds, pillars of entrances 'protected' for some kind of gargoyles, monsters, deities that will make it difficult to cross, to the point where the sage really engages in total self-clarity: the obstacle is inside, is the 'self'… and original smile happens. It involves unconditional surrender without any pre-negotiation conditions, in chemistry of agape… unconditional to cosmic emptiness… equanimity… them… unknown becomes known, it is 'discovered' … as a self-mirror… Beyond Awareness………

Glossary: KEY Concepts, Words, Terms Definitions

We need to clarify the meaning of some words used in this system to facilitate Our communications, because in some cases are dissimilar of the average social concepts.

Words feed the intellectual mind, but this system is preparing to make **'evolving transformations'**, which occurred by physiological changes. That new reality will happen **if** applied in natural order: Coherence among acts, thoughts, and concepts is required.

Life becomes proportional to our own inner work and not by imposed hierarchy as in older paradigms. Every human being has the right to 'discover' new states of self-regulation to living healthier and joyful in cosmic freedom.

Awareness- the individual state of inner power with pristine wisdom, where, in addition to our physical existence, is real another dimension; Awareness is a pristine identity as essence of you

Axis- an electro-chemical path, where neurons carry information throughout the body to the central nervous system; a "flowing circuit of light," an image analogy of our essence

Being- refers to the whole reality of a person, the physical aspect with energetic realms and electromagnetic fields superimposed

Being Presence- neurological coherence occurring after achieving an increased thermal state; one of the stages and states of awareness

Boundless Awareness- signals of the non-local state, fed by High Intention; the resulting condition of Being is called by some: the Universal Mind, or the Zero Point

Brain plasticity- with healthy immune response is a possibility to chance, but also, by personal option, but has a price: Let go the educative habits that poison the dynamic balance of chemistry-hormones-neuronal pathways. Turn the myriad of senso perceptions that input daily life in your 'best allies' to make you, healthier in aware life, efficient in front of the daily challenges and, in sustainable states of inner joy - natural smiles

Creative plasticity- the flexible ability of brain activity that results in a high quality of productive work and art

Cognitive consciousness- response of the intellectual mind that focus attention in some task, event, circumstance

Courage- as English language accept, this word meaning a value in people that show in most occasion altruistic attitudes in difficult situations, however, in translation to the Spanish speakers at Mexico, the meaning change to be parallel to anger

Coagulation- Time needed of self-care to allow any improvement just self-opened inside, to be stored with safe quality and quantity of energies; average 24 to 48 hours of calm and prudent distance from sociocultural pressures are suggested, after be exposed to an opportunity of a real vivencia

Dantiem- the primal force of life energy centred in the lower abdomen (aka Tandem)

Development- first serious inner work in the system, for most participants is to accomplish the first trace/triad of the Enneagram wisdom with modern technology training

Empowerment- self-work creating a life of health, efficiency, and happiness

Energy spectrum- different frequencies, vibrations, waves in this universe; represent matter in least dense quality of presence

Enlightenment- state in which everything everywhere is One in universal-cosmic wisdom

Experiences are states that can be checked against a database of our personal memory in this life or past-life occurrences. This is different of "Vivencia" – a unique revelation – which it is the one moment in life in which there is NO database against which one can check what is happening

Fibonacci sequence- Fibonacci spiral is the pattern in nature by which all things grow, by adding what went before to what exists now. It progresses as 0 1 1 2 3 5 8 13 21 34 55, etc. It is Nature's way of modifying this ideal Golden Ratio with an individual starting point. The body grows in Fibonacci patterns, as do all living forms in some way (e.g. the nautilus shell which shows the pattern most visibly)

Five antennas-horns- areas of the brain as keys for Awareness and higher states of Being; points/doors where biology interacts with the internal energy paths

Flexibility- is the brain's plasticity, an inherent functionality of natural learning the most efficient pathways, ease of modification by evolving goals, without pressures to repeat the older traditions

Fractal mathematics- geometric designs that portray the universal relationship, fractal forms play as variations - duplicate copies of original mathematic seeds

Glia cells- Are in the nervous system all around the body. The cerebellum (the smaller, lower back part of the brain) has more glia cells than both of the two upper hemispheres and it is paramount in perceiving the gravitational field. Glias record and recover memories, help with spatial and time orientation, are involved in paranormal abilities, and are one of the first electrical signals in many brain nerve pathways; glia cells are bridges to the highest human potentials

High gamma- brainwave frequencies above 40 Hertz, found in people in enlightened states; can be as high as 126 Hertz (or more) with harmonic brainwaves resonant between them at different locations on the scalp

High Intention- This energy shapes our life's course, giving us new meaning and goals. Similarly, a galaxy sends out bursts of star formations, which are new products in the universe, new life forms; is High Will open perceptions to light and energies, as a quasar

High Will- Intense discipline and exercises are needed to extract this strong force, a special quality and level of inner power and awareness that changes and opens up one's perceptions

Higher consciousness- equivalent to Awareness (in some schools)

Higg Will – the Higg Bosons are subatomic particles that by friction with the space-time field, create mass and transport forces on the subatomic realms. First was explained at the middle of past century by Peter Higg. The mathematical concept was dismissed for inefficient behavior of his contemporaneous scientific society; actual is a Nobel Price / Higg Boson proved at LCAP-Ginevra

Inner Keys- inner work unlocks and opens doors of wisdom, using inner keys. We achieve states of higher awareness through these personal cues that can be recalled at will. For example, we define our axis in order to create a unique, personal Inner Key, to be used at will. Everyone can learn to interconnect the bodies of matter, energies, movements and dimensions through biological self-regulation, and functional flowing of energetic fields. The development of psycho-physiological inner keys allow bridging among dimensions

Intention- our thoughts are raw material (like dough) which need the fire of intention (energy) to transform that dough into bread. Intention is Energy. Energy flows where attention goes. If you identify your Intention daily, and keep it in mind all day, you will automatically act to fulfill that intention

'Intent' is a word choice between us in the system, meaning a clear focuses goal-purpose, sustained by personal force of life and commitment. To be capable to teach as Master on human evolution is one 'intent' of self-journey, where you will give to others only what you conquer and integrate psycho-physiologically in yourself

Knowledge- is information-data that we add to the bank of memory in this life. It is intellectual eruditions that do not have the inner power to be an owner as in a 'vivencia'

Light - the energy of Awareness; the Light Body is composed of photons, the spectrum from red to violet in the display of universal energies; the primordial Light Force of the process of dimensional creation from the pristine dark cosmos; the origin from matter-antimatter universes

Life Force- one of the three primordial forces of this multidimensional universe, is corresponding on Physics analogies with dark matter, such as enveloped protector of planetary and humans matters-energies

Meridian- It is a preferred path where energy moves. Chi travels and is distributed to the body through these channels. The twelve principal meridians are named after the organs (such as liver, gall bladder, spleen, stomach.) This unique form of energy (Righteous Chi) is capable of integrating and providing vital nourishment, leading us into another dimension of Awareness by interact with the 8 extra-meridians / second skin. Besides physical anatomy, the spine is also the location of the central energetic meridian. Acupuncture points lie on these channels or rivers of energy as doors to access the possibility to modify the quantity and quality of the energetic flow (Chi - Qi - Ki)

Monkey Mind- is called the wild, noisy and disruptive mind with mundane thoughts. This superficial thinking mind, lacks control, and is occupied with insubstantial topics, habits and feelings. The wild animal mind engages in impulsive, undisciplined mental responses. Compulsive and addictive behaviors originate here. With intention and training the Monkey Mind can become a Pet Monkey / Pet Mind. Through observation you can intercept, and/or feed the Monkey a 'banana' Biofeedback training, metaphors, mantras, affirmations, breathing, and other self-care, self-development practice work together to tame the noisy non-productive Monkey Mind

Movement Force - one of the three primordial forces of this multidimensional universe, analogic of expansion-dark energy. This is the force with maximum speed in bring Higg Will evolving results, and for this reason intentional integrative movements done in teamwork at the system, are foundational for fast self-evolution

Neuroplasticity- the brain's ability to change and be flexible and responsive to new learning, thoughts, quality of will and intention (see Flexibility)

Optimal performance- a balanced, efficient state of healthy quality of life and a joyful personal life of success accomplished by self-inner work

Ordinary woman / man- in the ancient alchemy language are people that by innate reality they preserved a proportion of universal values, and are self-sufficient to ground in a healthy, free life, with almost soft inner joy

Original smile – A Buddhist expression that describes the pristine state of transcendence where human essence is beyond matter form in a realm of infinite possibilities; it is the starting point of universal life

Perceptions- are moments when the Observer is focused on something with the totality of his/her sensory tools, that is, the physical or energetic aspects of life (the five senses, the hands, the second skin, red alert at somatic information, etc.)

The HIKE system differentiates between "**seeing**" and "**looking**". "**Seeing**" is a physiological activity defined as photons that touch the retina in the eyes, while "**looking**" has a verbal component that reveals the recognition of an object from the database of memory. "**To watch**" is an intentional act of the mind to understand something

Phi ratio / Golden Mean / Golden Proportion- it is one universal mathematical relationship; can be viewed as an essential key of self-evolution with multiple levels of expression

Pristine field- (original, pure) program /movement/ Inner Song; our essence in the highest human expression

Pristine program, according to the system, is a natural flow of well-being in human life, universal software of always improving efficient outcomes, innate on the stem cells, DNA. The birthright to being healthy, efficient, and happy –here and now– is possible to attain through a balanced psychophysiology and an energetic field of high-quality vibration

Psychophysiology- the physical body function as it is influenced by mind, emotion, and immune system-. A more complex explanation than "mind-body"

Quantum Field continuity / Universal Mind / Quantum Mind / Universal Mind / Zero Point Field- the original and only universal energy field of pure infinite potentials

Quantum Observer- the "observer effect" in physics is: Focus intention in seeing is creating. "The Observer of an experiment can alter what happens in the laboratory because the Observer's influence the Quantum field." (Schrodinger's cat)

Raw spectrum of EEG- histogram display of all the individual frequencies of the EEG signal showing the rhythmic increases and decreases in height (power/amplitude)

Sendero Luminoso- Spanish's words that translated meaning 'pathway with light.' Were used in older alchemy language to ask for an efficient way of reaching freedom

Soul is the library of the past life memories, engaged in the electromagnetic field morphologic. The west door of Safe Place at the right timing allows decoding the different language of that data, and recovery of the information is a birthright of each human being. Intellectual mind speak by words in the grammar of the place-time that the subject is living, and soul signals are dissimilar pieces of the spectrum of energies that require some inner work, which activate subtle connections among glias, cerebellum, and spinal fluid. Soul is the energetic record that reconnects us to our past experiences, wisdom, and ultimately back to Universal Mind

Spirit- the light energy in photons (particle-waves) as presence of the Universal Mind on us

Synesthesia- the ability to perceive multiple sensory information / experiences at the same time beyond usual psychological reference; allows opening the electro-magnetic field to increase personal perceptions and facilitate new physiologic pathways

Tara- feminine form of Buddha, she is applied in many daily practices of that oriental religion; most common forms are white, green, red, and blue Tara
Three-legs- the axis line energetically extends from the head, down to the back of the sacrum, through the two physical legs. It is this tail an additional energetic path extending into/to the ground

Torus- a geometric shape; the logarithmic spiral in Phi Ratio. Humans have an energetic field in the shape of a torus: a pattern of unity in a spiral sequence that links to the core of the axis. This torus kernel-nature-essence is in each person as the reality of the bodies-forces-realms nested within. The torus pattern is one of the most evolved states of Awareness / Being

Transformation- the upward spiral of evolution beginning at the simplest level, to the joy experienced in psycho-physiological self-regulation, and to transcendent states of being. The system offered here practices that allowing owner the 4 legs as 'centaurs' with chemistries of agape, oxytocin, and unconditional equanimity self-regulated

Transmutation- one possible inner work where alchemy is practice as self-regulation of matters-energies states; the alchemy inner work of the second and beyond triad/trace of the Enneagram wisdom, with the support of biofeedback and neurofeedback plus the myriad of details that each person self-regulated in self, by real commitment and clarity

Transmission- realm of teaching only used by advanced masters, most basic common style is dream work

Universal Wisdom- the collective a-temporal wisdom from all the souls of all life forms in the universe and beyond

Unknown Keys work in triangles-tetrahedrons in golden mean proportions that engage-relate-coordinate the capacity of the Ring of Singularity-Dantiem. That area is called also the lake of the belly, plus the Pearl of Light in the heart shining in harmony with the Unicorn point, guides the dynamic flow of energies-forces

Vivencia does not have a database, it is a new, undisclosed moment of total presence in a never before lived situation. "Vivencia" – a unique revelation – which it is the one moment in life in which there is NO database against which one can check what is happening

Wisdom is a dynamic, a-temporal process where the information-data universal is integrated beyond the intellectual memory bank with all the correlations, and it is available at High Will of the sage-seeker to be applied as response to life, with coherent actions in this dimension-time

Wonder- in the Human Inner Keys for Evolution system I was research, during 50 years, 7 different states of enlightens, from the 'original smile,' to the 'BE One with'…, 'open wings,' etc. 'Wonder' is one of these as self-regulated reality of living in the awe of the psychophysiology of elixirs, having a healthy long life of manifest peace, joy, and evolving outcomes for this humanity and planet.

Biographies

Balpreda, Silvia

Silvia was born in Santa Fe, Argentina. She has two wonderful children. She taught in Buenos Aires for 10 years until 1995, when she moved with her family to the United States, where she later became a citizen. Silvia lived in state of Michigan for 30 years and for one year in Colorado.
In the United States, she worked as a Spanish Teacher for several years in schools and privately tutored professionals. In 2003 started in social work. She served as a Family Support specialist for Easter Seals in programs that addressed infant brain development, emotional development, and communication skills. Her work focused on healthy mother-infant attachment and the prevention of child abuse and neglect. In 2010, Silvia was honored on International Women's Day by the Metropolitan International Institute of Detroit as a Distinguished American-Argentine Citizen for her valuable contributions to the American community and society. In 2024, Silvia moved to Barcelona, Spain, where she continued her studies with Dr. Liana Mattulich, which she had begun in Buenos Aires in 1979. She is filled with curiosity and strong commitment to life-long learning and understanding more life beyond common consciousness and awareness.

Correa, Lucrecia M

Born in Argentina, Lucrecia is proud of the public school system in her country, always demonstrating solidarity among peers, students, and teachers. Mother of two sons. She moved to the USA and completed her career in ESL at the University of Minnesota.

She taught in schools in Minneapolis and Denver, CO, where she met Dr. Liana Mattulich and began a new path in self-development and practice of Neurofeedback and Biofeedback.

During her time in Minneapolis, she gained deep human insight through her work at Hennepin County Medical Center, where all races, languages, and religions intersect in this part of the world.

Dorna, Lizette M. Ph.D.

Lizette M. Dorna, Ph. D., is a Clinical Psychologist from San Juan, Puerto Rico. She received her Doctor's degree in 2009 from the University of Puerto (UPR), Río Piedras Campus. Her doctoral dissertation was on "The Effect of Neurofeedback on the Attention of Eight Puerto Rican College Students". She has presented her research at various professional associations including the Association for Applied Psychophysiology and Biofeedback (AAPB) and the Puerto Rico Psychology Association (APPR). She did her clinical internship in neuropsychology in the Neurology Department of the University District Hospital, Río Piedras Medical Center in 2005-2006. She also served as Executive Director of the Liceo Oriental Psicológico (Psychological Oriental Institute) from 2003 to 2014.

Dr. Dorna's interest in Neurofeedback dates back to 1999, when she met Dr. Liana Mattulich and took her first neurofeedback training with her. It was a very powerful experience that motivated her to pursue further studies and training under Dr. Mattulich's mentorship. She has since collaborated and assisted her in different capacities.

Fajardo Bonza, Deyba

From a very young age in her native Colombia, Deyba was always fascinated by human anatomy, especially the brain capacity and its potential. She sought information after having extrasensory experiences as a child, but had no luck. She always believed that every person has these abilities. At 17, she moved to Miami, where she met Dr. Liana Mattulich. From that moment on, she learned and practiced biofeedback techniques, brainwave training, metaphors, and Dr. Liana's teachings, which changed her life forever. They not only facilitated her academic education but also her personal growth. Today, Deyba has 26 years of practice in Traditional Chinese Medicine, Acupuncture, and other therapies. She has facilitated several retreats with Dr. Liana in various locations around the world, integrating both techniques with fabulous results.

This is the perfect moment, here and now, to be and live in the eternal present and cultivate the practice of personal and global growth and evolution. For the good of every human being and the well-being of all. These tools are the most effective vehicle to achieve this goal and this challenge.

Contact information: Deybaacuwellness@gmail.com

Hambleton, Ann

All aspects of the universe have frequencies. Liana Mattulich's work with neurofeedback training and meditation as well as her design of a cutting-edge neurofeedback program to elevate the frequencies of the brain allows individuals to evolve to higher states of consciousness. Ann has studied and been mentored by Liana for many years, focusing on the teachings, exercises and meditations. Her background includes eastern and western herbology, Japanese five element and Chinese acupuncture which involves discerning patterns of energy imbalances. She graduated with degrees in biology and anthropology with an emphasis on ethnobotany. Also in her quiver is biodynamic gardening which acknowledges the influence of various planets effects on plants.
Currently Ann lives in northeastern Washington state. She and her husband have a 45 acre farm in the mountains and practice regenerative techniques. Ann's particular interest is in perennial medicinal herb beds. She continues to study alternative healing methods to raise frequencies of individuals and optimize health.

Hawkes, Alistair M MA, LPC

Alistair M. Hawkes is a licensed psychotherapist who specializes in guiding fellow therapists, art professionals, and corporates executives to find inner peace and higher dynamic creativity to fly beyond awareness, using the HIKE4evolution™ system. She is passionate about helping others, persistent in a fault, and loves to learn.
Alistair is available to speak on stage and do media interviews. She loves to share on topics that focus on providing these leaders with actionable insights and tools to address and prevent burnout, and distress, creating their best lives. This ensures they can continue to provide effective outcomes and success, while maintaining their own well-being.
When the alchemy transformation is your next opportunity, there will be another young master who, with the highest compassion (he does not use a band-aid but is one 'expert' on the amputation of any gangrenes), offers

efficient outcomes with his humble presence of never-ending wisdom. As a teamwork global coordinator, open to your goals new fountains of unique vivencias, practices, movements, etc., which the system offers worldwide.
She can be contacted at: https://www.alistairmhawkes.com/

Hawkes, Dallas R, M.S. - Applied Mathematics

Dallas Hawkes is an ordinary man. As a long-time seeker of a deeper understanding of the power of faith, logic and intent, Dallas has been a student of various martial arts and body movement systems, Native American prayer services and mathematics. Body movement helped create healthy boundaries and flexibility. Mathematics taught abstract thought. Spending time with the original people of this land integrated the importance of community, where real change happens, if dedicated.
He has been highly trained in the use of bio-neurofeedback by Dr. Liana Mattulich, MD (Argentina), pioneer on scientific feedback to open 'wings' -human higher potentials.
Using technology in ways taught by the HIKE4Evolution™ system has accelerated the integration of many experiences of his life leading to a clear, sustainable vision of becoming more humane together.

He can be contacted: https://hike4evolution.com/contact/

Mattulich, Liana MD, CEEG, BCIAC

Dr. Liana Mattulich became a physician at the School of Medicine of the University of Buenos Aires, Argentina, in 1963, providing medical and preventive care. She was a pioneer in biofeedback from 1973 and, in 1980, the Founder and Director of the Biofeedback Center of Buenos Aires.

Moved to USA become citizen; In Colorado since 1995, Founder LABA (Latin chapter of the Association for Applied Psychophysiology and Biofeedback - AAPB). A Fellow of BCIAC and certified in EEG, she was president of CAAPB 1998-2001. Also, Dr. Liana Mattulich organized with Dr. Sharon Montes the one-month practice of Biofeedback and Neurofeedback for students of Medicine of the University of Colorado, Department of Family Medicine.

For over 25 years, she has practiced and taught Zen, Tibetan meditations, and exercises from native South American cultures and the Sufis, all of which she has incorporated into her professional work. After years of retreat in a Buddhist monastery, she realized the need to become a bridge between the scientific approach and ancient wisdom; she made this possible with the Foundation of the Inner Key System.

Dr. Liana is now retired from social activities and lives in the Rocky Mountains. She continues to support the national and international core team of Human Inner Keys for Evolution/NASSAQ in the fields of matters-energies and forces.

Montes, Sharon MD

Dr Sharon Montes, is an internationally recognized pioneer in the field of integrative health and holistic medicine She has over 35 years of clinical and teaching experience. She served as Medical Director for such prestigious health care facilities as: The University of Maryland Center for Integrative Medicine; Rose and AF Williams Family Medicine Centers – University of Colorado; and The School of Medicine; Arlington Community Health Center. She also operated an active clinical practice while teaching students, residents, and other practitioners.

Dr. Montes continues her international role of lecturer, course director, and radio and TV subject matter expert. Audiences include physicians, residents, nurses, allied and complementary health providers, patients, direct care groups, and community members. She is Founder of Living Well Whole Health, working with others together to integrate the wisdom of science and spirit to support optimal Whole Health of mind-body-spirit. For over 30 years, Dr. Montes has been an advocate of Integrative Functional Medicine – the combination of Western, Eastern, and Lifestyle Medicines, and Epigenetics (the study of genes.

Her current focus is using integrative functional medicine to help people prevent and reverse cognitive decline. In addition she, continues to mentor and coach fellow doctors in using integrative functional medicine to optimize their personal health.

She can be reached at: www.livingwellwholehealth.com/brainhealth LinkedIn presence https://www.linkedin.com/in/sharondmontesmd/

Liana Mattulich MD, CEEG, BCIAC

PS note from Liana:

Written by me in alchemy language, the illustrations are done by Dallas Hawkes, but the credit for editing this book, --as a grammatical version of correct idiom, plus open clarity in the ideas-information-pearls exposes in this uncommon style --learning to learn, are totally the manifestation of two 'miracle editors' Sharon Montes, and Alistair Hawkes, and… in so fast time!... speed of light cosmic… … …

Mahalo, thank you, muchas gracias, arigato for read these pages… … …
*** *** ***
--- Liana 2025

CONTACT US

These teachings are universal and extend beyond social cultural boundaries. They provide an efficient distillation and blending of Cutting-Edge Technology and Elixirs of Wisdom. This system allows everybody to invest a few minutes daily to reach your goals, rather than longer hours each day for many years. The planet needs you to enjoy a healthy efficient life. Please radiate and echo these qualities.

NASSAAQ is derived from an Inuit word that means
A Voyage to Discovery. This journey includes
Self-regulation is the pathway.
Self-responsibility is the way to reach to
Amplify human highest potentials of
Awareness and
Quality of personal life.

https://NASSAAQ.com

Appendix

1. Golden Mean Field

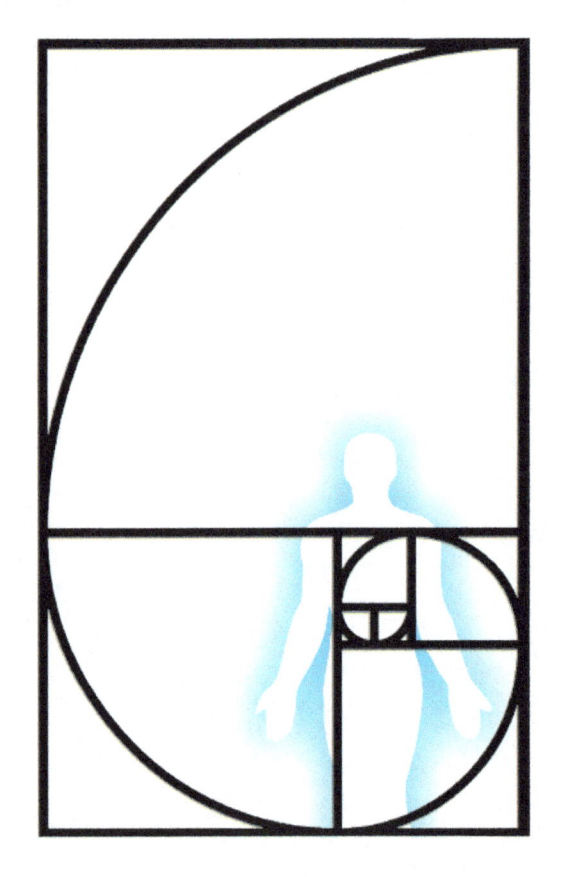

2. Golden Mean Spiral with Numbers

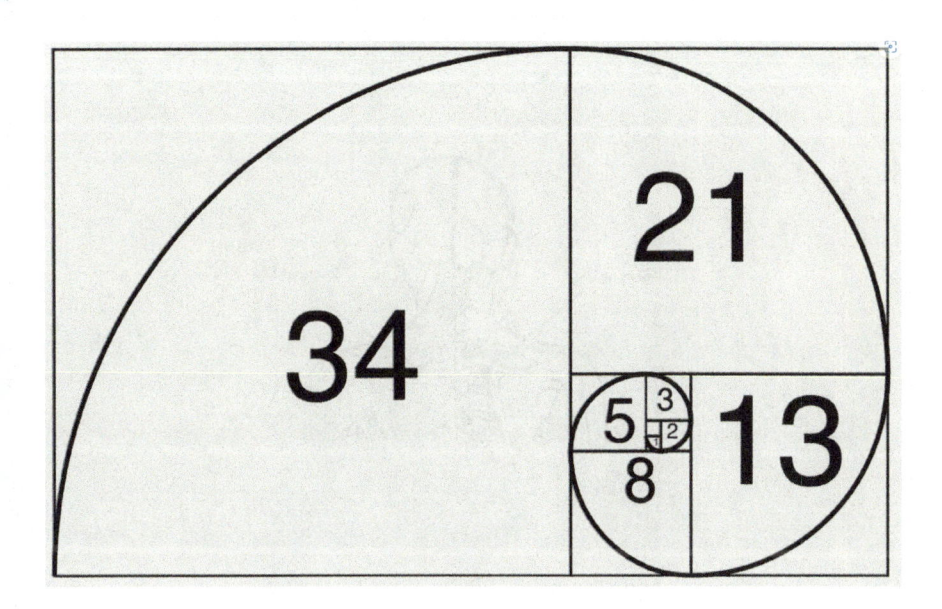

3. Meridian Points

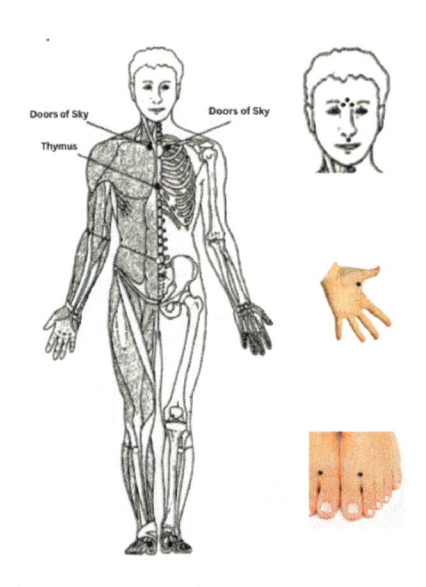

130

4. Awareness Points

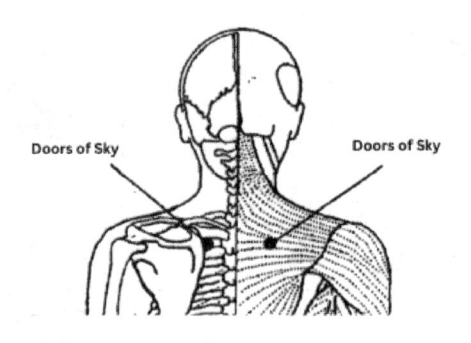

5. Enneagram

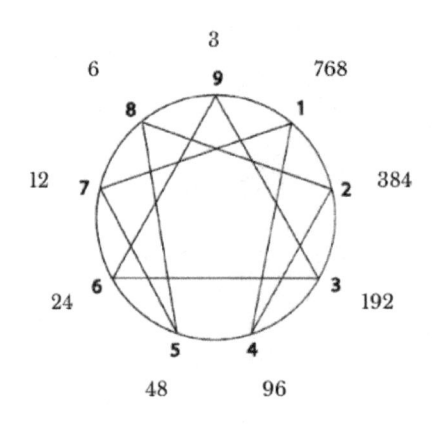

6. Toroidal Field

7. Top View of Wisdom Centers

Top View of 4 Legs/4 Antennae

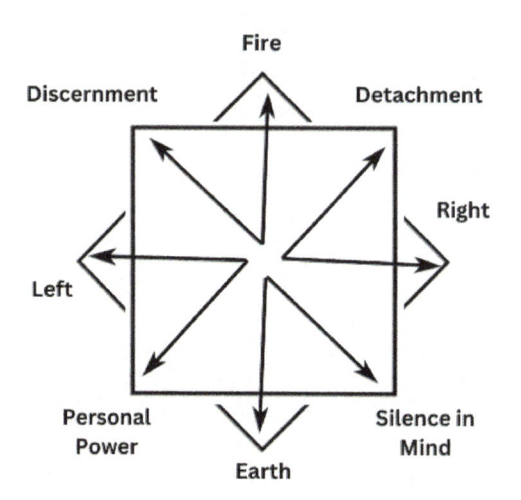

- Fire
- Discernment
- Detachment
- Right
- Left
- Personal Power
- Silence in Mind
- Earth

8. Pathways of Wisdom Connections

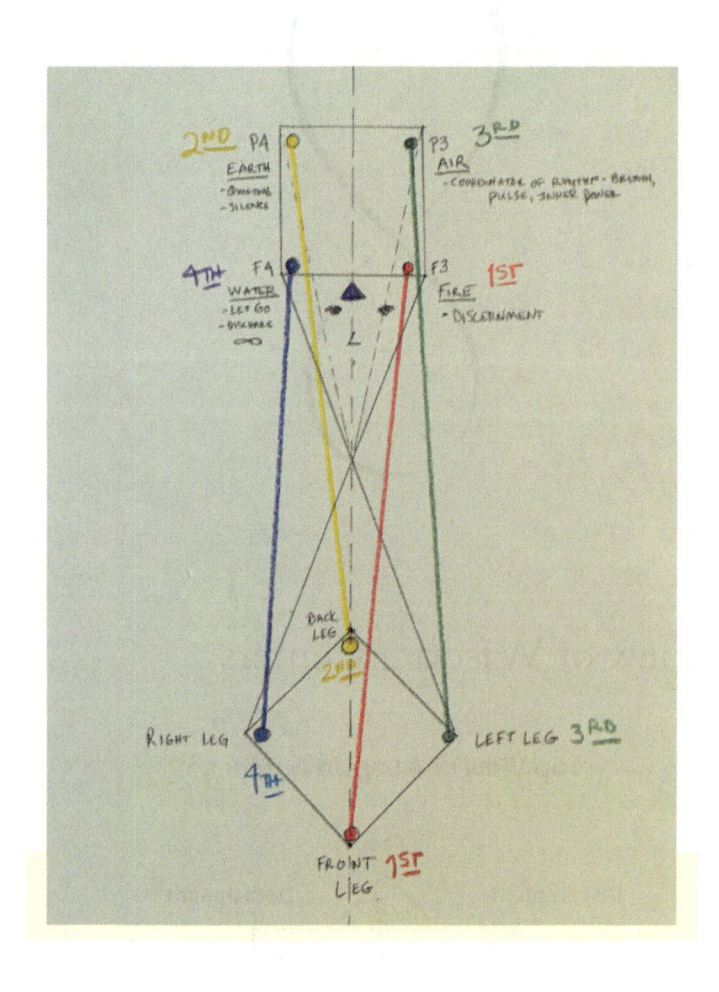

Made in the USA
Las Vegas, NV
01 May 2025

21583418R00085